British Touring Car Racing

IN CAMERA

British Touring
Car Racing
IN CAMERA
A PHOTOGRAPHIC
CELEBRATION OF 50 YEARS

Graham Robson

First published in March 2008

A catalogue record for this book is available from the British Library

ISBN 978 1 84425 469 9

Library of Congress catalog card no. 2007943086

Haynes North America Inc., 861 Lawrence Drive, Newbury Park, California 91320, USA

Published by Haynes Publishing, Sparkford, Yeovil, Somerset BA22 7JJ, UK. Tel: 01963 442030 Fax: 01963 440001 Int. tel: +44 1963 442030 Int. fax: +44 1963 440001 E-mail: sales@haynes.co.uk Website: www.haynes.co.uk

Printed and bound in Britain by J. H. Haynes & Co. Ltd, Sparkford, Yeovil, Somerset BA22 7JJ

All photographs from the author's collection apart from:
Halfords 198-199, 200 top
Roger Lane 40-41, 47, 48, 49 top, 69 bottom, 72-73
LAT Photographic 74-75, 79-83, 84 top, 105-113, 133, 135-139
Prodrive 184-187
Paul Skilleter 16, 20-21, 22 top, 24 bottom, 26-27
Sutton Motorsport 178-181
Vauxhall 188-189, 209-233
Volvo 190-193

ACKNOWLEDGEMENTS

Because this book covers well over 50 years, I have needed to assemble images and information from experts, and from many libraries and collections, so I would now like to breathe a big 'thank you' to them all:

Roger Bell, John Blunsden, Ray Baker, BMW UK, Ralph Broad, Jeremy Browne, Peter Browning, Peter Darley, John Davenport, Vic Elford, Ferret Photography, Ford Photographic Archive (in particular Dave Hill), Halfords, Jaguar, Roger Lane (Agfa in the 1960s), LAT (which includes *The Autocar* from many years ago), Richard Longman, Rob Lyall, Alan Mann, Andy Middlehurst, MG-Rover, Win Percy, Bill Price, Prodrive, Paul Radisich, John Rhodes, Andy Rouse, SEAT Motorsport (and particularly Paul Evans), Ken Shipley, Paul Skilleter (and *Jaguar World*), Sutton Images, Ian Titchmarsh, Toyota GB, Stuart Turner, Jeff Uren, Vauxhall Heritage (and Andrew Duerden), Volvo Car UK

– all of whom had special memories of the series in which they were involved from time to time.

GRAHAM ROBSON, 2008

CONTENTS

Author's Introduction 7

EARLY DAYS — Jaguar domination in the 1950s 8

1958–1965 — Constant rule changes 18

1966–1969 — Anything goes... 44

1970–1973 — Group 2 76

1974–1982 — Group 1, and Group '1½' 92

1983–1990 — Group A, with real power 114

1991–2000 — Super Touring cars 140

2001–2007 — Modern times 194

British Championship Results 234

Index 238

Fifty years ago the British Racing & Sports Car Club (the BRSCC) promoted the original British Saloon Car Championship. Although the competing cars always looked exciting, in the beginning their performance was quite modest, though competition was always fierce. But that was then, and this is now.

It was only when I looked back to the first saloon car races that I ever witnessed – at Silverstone in May 1955, to be precise – that I realised how much, how far, and how completely what is now officially known as 'Touring Car' racing has changed in half a century. Today's tightly-regulated 2-litre machines are vastly more sophisticated than their ancestors, more capable and, of course, much more controllable.

Although I didn't actually see Britain's very first saloon car race, which took place at Silverstone in 1952, I have been a fan of this exciting type of motor sport since that time. The ever-increasing speed of the cars, the advances in technology, and the sheer colourful nature of the machines themselves made that inevitable.

Amazingly, it took some years for the authorities, and indeed every motor racing enthusiast, to take saloon racing seriously. Until the mid-1960s the British Championship was promoted only by the British Racing & Sports Car Club. The RAC MSA took up the reins in 1966, and has held control – lately under a franchise agreement – ever since then.

I was delighted to get the opportunity to compile a history of this type of racing, but soon discovered that, over the years, there had been so many changes of regulations that many illustrations would be needed to tell a coherent story. It was, in other words, easier to emphasise the sheer majesty of Jim Clark's driving in a picture than in purple prose, easier to show off the variety and amazing performance of 500bhp Group A cars in images rather than in words, and to cram the pages concerning 1990s-style

Super Touring Car Championships with pictures rather than dull race reports.

But, do I have a favourite period? It's difficult to answer that one, particularly as it was sometimes difficult to compare the different decades. Although I witnessed many an epic 'battle of the Jaguars' in the 1950s, it was the three-wheeling Lotus-Cortina antics of heroes like Jim Clark in the 1960s which really got me going.

As a young *Autocar* reporter I was close to the Group 5 scene of the 1960s, where I found the high-tech approach of some team bosses quite awe-inspiring, but like many of my friends I was less enthralled by Group '1½' which followed in the 1970s, where one really needed a Ford Capri 3000GT or a Rover SD1 to make it to the victory rostrum.

Group A in the 1980s was real, full-on, high-power, tyre-stripping stuff, and the fact that Ford's mighty Sierra RS500 Cosworths came to dominate for so long was really due to a lack of credible competition from any of the rival manufacturers. The reaction – to impose a 2-litre Super Touring Cars formula for the 1990s was so successful that many new manufacturers came on board, produced great cars – then discovered that there was a cost, and retired to soothe their bruised balance sheets.

All of this, then, led to the modern formula, where many components and specifications are controlled, in an attempt to contain costs. Unhappily, though, these cars are not nearly as fast as the Super Tourers that they replaced, which leaves many Old Hands to bemoan what they are still missing.

It is the images, rather than the words, which make this such a revealing 50-year history, and I hope I have been able to find the best examples to tell a complete story. To do that, though, I had to tap many helpful sources, and what follows tells its own story ...

Graham Robson
Spring 2008

Looking back, it's difficult to realise that serious saloon car races were not held in Britain before 1952, and that there was no coherent British Saloon Car Championship before 1958. Before then, it seems, saloon car racing was not thought to be credible, as there were very few truly fast cars to make the races exciting. Races for road-going sports cars were, at least, taken seriously, but not for normal road-going saloons.

Way back, it seems, the rather tongue-in-cheek tone had been set in 1938, when a 'one-make' Fiat 500 (Topolino) race had been held at Brooklands – when Britain's loftiest 'establishment' motoring magazine, *The Autocar*, had treated the spectacle with raised eyebrows and a great deal of forced jollity: 'Overjoyed enthusiasts of Brooklands had looked forward to this for weeks. Pieces of cheese on strings had been prepared as bait, and there was talk of releasing a cat behind the machines at the start...'

No-one seemed to care much about preparation, there was no excitement in the event itself, and no-one felt interested in trying again. Even so: 'At the start the whole bunch of little cars screamed down the straight together, over-revving scandalously, and more bumping and boring took place at the first corner than ever before...'

Somehow this sounds familiar, even by 1990s and 2000s standards! For the record, it was S. Mond who won the 4.5-mile race, just 0.2 seconds ahead of C.B. Phillips, at an average speed of 42.45mph. In the future, things could only get faster.

All this, therefore, may explain why saloon car racing was not seriously considered before the 1950s, especially as very few British cars could yet exceed 100mph (before the Jaguar Mk VII came on to the scene, it was the Riley-engined Healeys that set most of the standards).

Soon after the Second World War, in any case, where Britain as a nation was still war-battered and effectively bankrupt, there was a dire shortage of competitive machinery, especially as automotive imports (of racing cars, and of road cars) were still officially banned. What this meant is that when motor sport seriously got under way once again (Silverstone's first-ever race was held in 1948), any sort of racing, for any sort of modern cars was welcome.

This led to racing for 'production' cars being introduced at first, but in the first few years such events made no attempt to separate open two-seaters from other types, which meant that Jaguar XK120s would be pitted against Riley RM saloons, Jowett Jupiters, and even Ford Zephyrs. The first of what proved to be trend-setting 'production car' races was held at Silverstone in August 1949, when 'works' Jaguar XK120s took first (Leslie Johnson) and second (Peter Walker) places from Norman Culpan's Frazer Nash. The winner's speed over this 1-hour race was 82.18mph, while the best saloon car performance was set by B. Mylchreest's Riley RMC 2½-litre saloon, at 65.94mph.

As S.C.H. 'Sammy ' Davis, that much respected Sports Editor of *The Autocar*, later commented: 'To me the production car race stands out a mile – it was just what we wanted to see and gave a real idea of the possibilities of most of the cars we thought about. It really didn't matter a bit who won. It was just a good practical demonstration. The next race of this type ought to be very carefully organised, and the cars ought to be as near as possible stock...'

Those wanting to win in early events, therefore, prepared out-and-out two-seater sports cars, and although all sort of odd, sometimes handicap, events were held at club level, it was not until 10 May 1952 that the very first post-war International saloon-car-only race was held at Silverstone – in the *Daily Express* meeting. For a time, this was merely a once-in-a-year event, and surprisingly it was not immediately copied by any other promoter at any other circuit.

Massive, tyre-squealing 'works' Jaguar Mk VIIs dominated that first event, just as they would always do for the first five years. Stirling Moss won the 17 lap race at 75.22mph (fastest lap 2min. 18sec/76.36mph), though Ken Wharton (Healey Elliott, with 2½-litre Riley engine) ran him close.

Naturally there was keen competition in the smaller-engined capacity classes, but since much of the opposition came from more expensive sports saloons – like the Bristols, Healeys, Sunbeam-Talbots, Riley 2½-litres, Jowett Javelins and MG models – there was no interest from Ford or Vauxhall, whose cars were not then batting in the same performance league.

Small cars like Austin A30s, Morris Minors and side-valve Anglias might have been amusing to watch at this time, but were hopelessly underpowered – even when the regulations allowed them to use alternative cylinder heads.

In 1953, as in 1952, there was nothing to touch the Jaguars, so Stirling Moss came out to play in the self-same Mk VII that had won in 1952 (a car which spent most of its otherwise blameless life as a factory development car, and was therefore very non-standard in some ways, though no-one really seemed to mind), being followed home by Riley RM 2½-litre, Alvis 3-litre, Healey Tickford and Bristol 401 types.

Even so, word among Britain's gentleman racers was getting around, that this was fun, so no fewer than seventeen different makes took the start in 1954, but as before it was Jaguar (three of them in line astern – Ian Appleyard, Tony Rolt and Stirling Moss) that led the way home. There was one important consequence to this result, when one-time Ford 'works' rally driver Ford dealer Ken Wharton, who never got to drive a 'works' Jaguar, then sat down to read the Silverstone race's rules very carefully – and entered a remarkably rapid 2.3-litre Zephyr for the 1955 *Daily Express* event.

This was a classic case (as Stirling Moss used to point out), of the competition beginning when the regulations arrived, for Wharton realised just how much modification was allowed, and produced a car that was extremely non-standard. Sporting homologation, as such, had not yet been invented, and it was really the organisers' fault that such latitude was allowed.

Because the six-cylinder Zephyr was in the 2.0–3.0-litre class, which included a trio of newly-developed 2½-litre Riley Pathfinders, it was clear that Wharton was not just looking to beat them, but to pulling well clear, and was aiming to make a challenge to the Jaguars too!

On this occasion it was Raymond Mays (of ERA and BRM race car fame) whose tuning business had worked wonders on the six-cylinder engine, and with Wharton behind the wheel the car really flew. With more than

100bhp from the engine (that doesn't sound much today, but in 1955 it was a creditable output), and with stiffened-up suspension, this had all the makings of a formidable saloon racer.

In fact the Zephyr's chase was in vain, for no-one could catch the big Jaguars, but the big Ford tangled successfully with the Rileys (which, as road tests proved, were really much faster in normal road-car form), taking a class lead on the fifth of 25 laps, and swept home in fourth place overall. Mike Hawthorn's winning Jaguar Mk VIIM averaged 78.95mph, while Wharton's Zephyr averaged 76.18mph – a remarkable achievement. Interestingly enough, Tony Brookes's 2-stroke DKW won the 1-litre class at 67.66mph, and Dick Jacobs's MG ZA Magnette the 1,500cc class at 71.45mph, so there was interest right down the order.

This, at last, opened the floodgates to other enterprising teams, manufacturers and tuners. For 1956 Wharton dropped the Zephyr in favour of a 2.6-litre Austin A90 Westminster, and the new, larger-engined, 2.6-litre Zephyr Mk IIs would not be competitive again until 'works' assistance became available. Nothing, in any case could touch the Jaguars at this period of history, where factory-prepared Mk VIIs and Mk VIIMs (of which we now know that at least one of the 'works' cars had a full aluminium body shell !) always ruled the roost, especially if team manager 'Lofty' England had ensured that they were steered by 'works' D-Type drivers.

By this time, in case, Jaguar had become even more dominant, for in 1957 their drivers at the *Daily Express* meeting were supplied with the latest 3.4 saloons. Because these used the same twin-cam XK engines as the Mark VIIs and VIIMs had always done, but ran in body structures that were smaller, sleeker, lighter and more nimble – they were quite uncatchable by any of their opposition. That was the year in which Mike Hawthorn's 'works' 3.4 won the 15 lap race at 82.19mph (it lapped in 2min 5sec/84.3mph – 13 seconds faster than Moss's Mk VII had achieved just five years earlier).

Ford Zephyrs had a good and flamboyant tilt at the 3-litre class, but it wasn't enough, as they were no match for 'Gib' Grace's Riley Pathfinder, Ron Flockhart's 2.4-litre or Jack Sears's Austin A105 Westminster, while the first portents of the future came when John Sprinzel's Austin A35 finished close behind the DKW in the 1-litre class. This was the first time that a BMC A-Series engine had figured in a saloon car race – but it was merely the first of many such occasions.

As *The Autocar*'s staff reported after that race, 'One special joy of the Silverstone spectator is the sight of a car like his own being driven flat out by someone else, with the knowledge that it is not his worry if it blows up...'

This might be one reason why one of Britain's leading race organisers, the British Racing and Sports Car Club (BRSCC), decided to promote a series of saloon car races at its own meetings in 1958. With FIA homologation rules now in place, and with the ability to have all cars competing against each other on similar technical terms, the BRSCC decided to promote all events, nationwide.

Thus it was that, for 1958, the original BRSCC Saloon Car Championship was to be held.

50 YEARS OF PROGRESS

It's interesting to look back to the 1950s, and to work out just how, and where, touring cars got so much faster in half a century.

Engine power
The most powerful Jaguar Mk VIIMs had about 200bhp from 3.4 litres, with Zephyrs and A90s aiming for 130–150bhp, and small cars like the Austin A35 and 850 Minis having up to 75bhp. By the late 1960s, 1-litre Fords had up to 120bhp, 1.6-litre Lotus-Cortinas 180bhp and American Fords between 400bhp and 500bhp. To win in the 1970s one needed 500bhp in a Chevrolet Camaro, and in the 1980s, 550bhp in a Ford Sierra RS500 Cosworth. A reversion to 2-litre engines, and strict regulations, pegged back the limits to about 300bhp in the 1990s, and perhaps to only 270bhp in the 2000s.

Power/weight ratio
The following are estimates, but (I hope) shrewd ones, and this is where a comparison is telling. A 1950s-type Jaguar Mk VIIM disposed of about 120bhp/tonne, which was enough to win races, while a Jaguar 3.8 Mk II probably raised that to 160bhp/tonne. Ford's Galaxie shattered that, at more than 250bhp/tonne, as did the agile Lotus-Cortina due to its light weight. Chevrolet Camaros certainly had more than 300bhp/tonne. Later, the 3-litre Capris, which won everything in the 1970s, were relatively underpowered because of more engine restrictions, with little more than 220bhp/tonne at best. Then came the colossally powerful Ford Sierra RS500 Cosworths of the late 1980s, whose 555bhp engines gave them at least 420–430bhp/tonne. Super Touring Cars of the late 1990s were all restricted to well under 300bhp/tonne, although their chassis abilities made up for it, and the modern 21st century variety are even less powerful than that.

Brakes
Early Jaguars, Ford Zephyrs and even Austin A35s had to use their drum brakes sparingly, to prevent fade on longer events. Disc brakes were first found on Jaguar Mk IIs in 1958 (all four wheels), on cars as various as the Mini-Coopers, Sunbeam Rapiers, Ford Cortina GTs and Lotus-Cortinas (all front wheels only) from the early 1960s, after which four-wheel discs either became standard, or were homologated as kits, for all but the lightest of cars in the 1970s. The powerful Ford Falcons, Galaxies and Chevrolet Camaros coped with all demands from the 1970s, while Sierra RS500 Cosworths were very adequately braked in the 1980s. Thereafter braking ceased to be a factor.

Tyres
The first racing saloons just blew up their road rubber and hoped for the best, or fitted Michelin X tyres if the right size was available. 1960s Group 5 cars used whatever was available for single-seaters, but by the 1970s every tyre manufacturer was developing special tyres for the heavier, less wieldy 'tin tops'. Different constructions were available for different conditions, and every team had a specialist to advise them.

⬆ When Stirling Moss drove this factory-prepared Jaguar Mk VII to win the Silverstone touring car race of 1952, he established a tradition which would persist for a decade – until Jack Sears' massive Ford Galaxie upset all that in 1963.

⬅ Healey Elliotts like this were worthy 'class' cars in the 1950s, for even in standard road car form they could beat 100mph – but nothing could outpace the Jaguars of the day.

Same car, same driver, same circuit – but this was Silverstone in 1953, where Stirling Moss once again won the Touring Car race. In the intervening twelve months since 1952 this had been a hard-working test car at the Jaguar factory.

LWK 343 was a glutton for punishment, for it competed several times at Silverstone in the 1950s. Following victory in 1952 and 1953, it finished third in 1954, once again driven by Stirling Moss.

In 1955 Ken Wharton prepared the fastest Ford Zephyr yet seen on the tracks, and finished a magnificent fourth behind the usual Jaguar Mk VIIMs at Silverstone. This was the start of a long Ford love-affair with Touring Car Racing.

Pick your day, pick your class, and cross your fingers – this was Vic Derrington in a Ford Consul, fighting it out with Len Potter in a Peugeot 203. Not fast enough to win, but still good fun.

⬆ Plenty of variety here, with Desmond Titterington's 'works' Jaguar Mk VIIM sweeping past Michael Burn's two-stroke DKW on the inside.

↗ Some 'works' Jaguars were very versatile – this being PWK 700, driven by Tony Rolt in the 1954 Silverstone race, on its way to second place. Two years later the self-same car would win the Monte Carlo rally! We may guess – we may be sure – that the Ford Prefect 100E has been lapped, maybe more than once!

➡ One year on from 1955, and Ken Wharton thought he could out-do his gallant Ford Zephyr epic with this run in an Austin A90 Westminster. In 1956, he was vindicated – for this was the battle for outright victory, with Ivor Bueb's Mk VIIM, which the Jaguar eventually won by just one second – in 20 laps.

↖ Jaguar's fearsome, ill-handling 3.4 made its race debut at Silverstone in September 1957, where Ivor Bueb (this car) took third place behind Mike Hawthorn and Archie Scott-Brown in sister cars. Saloon car racers were getting slightly smaller – but faster.

← For spectators, the joy of saloon car racing came in the sheer variety of cars – here, in 1954, Ronnie Adams (privately-entered Jaguar Mk VII, leads Reg Parnell's Daimler Conquest Century, from another Century, with a Riley RMC tucked in close behind.

↑ Basil De Mattos in a Laystall-supported Ford Consul, ahead of Buckley's Bristol 403, at Silverstone in 1955.

The announcement came in January 1958, when *Autosport* carried an important news piece in its issue of 10 January. The British Racing & Sports Car Club (BRSCC) had finally seen the attractions of tin-top racing, and elected to run an 11-round Saloon Car Championship, with six of the events being run at Brands Hatch.

Although this series was not officially backed by Britain's motorsport authority (the RAC) at first, it was the forerunner of every other saloon series in this country. Originally the BRSCC stated that it would be for 'modified production cars', though it was also stressed that 'no major modifications, such as the alteration of the cylinder head or camshaft, will be permitted, but competitors will be encouraged to improve the road-holding of their cars by fitting anti-roll bars, and so forth.'

Entries were to be divided into four classes – up to 1,200cc, 1,201 to 1,600cc, 1,601 to 2,700cc, and over 2,700cc – with points being awarded by class, and not overall. Accordingly, as Gregor Grant pointed out, '…the competitor entering an Austin A35 stands as good a chance of winning the Championship as does the driver of a 3.4 Jaguar.'

Private-owner Jeff Uren (who had beaten all the 'works' Fords at Silverstone in 1957) astonished everyone by fighting head-to-head throughout the year with Jack Sears' BMC-backed Austin A105. These two drivers easily outscored all their rivals, and ended the season as the class act in the new Championship.

In those days the cars were relatively simple as Jeff Uren once confirmed: 'In 1957, apart from having the engine totally rebuilt, lightened, balanced and fitted with an SU instead of a downdraught Zenith carburettor, and in doing the best possible with revised suspension settings and brake materials, that was the size of it, and the 1958 car was not much more special.'

As usual, Jaguars won most races outright, but their efforts were overshadowed, the highlight of most events being usually the running battle between Jeff Uren's Zephyr and Sears' BMC-backed Austin A105 Westminster. Although Uren only started eight races, the Zephyr won its class three times and Sears six times.

After the final race at Brands Hatch in October, the result was that Sears and Tommy Sopwith (Jaguar 3.4) were tied at the top of the table, with no official way of separating them. So (and could this ever happen again?) the two were supplied with identical Riley 1.5s, which BMC had prepared at Abingdon, and sent out to race mano-a-mano for five laps, before swapping cars and doing it all again! One car, clearly, was slightly faster than the other – for Sears was fastest by four seconds in one race, and Sopwith by 2.2 seconds in the other, but using the same car. The Championship, by just 1.8 seconds, therefore went to Jack.

After this encouraging start, the BRSCC pressed ahead, liberalised the regulations, and saw a number of truly fast cars entered. In later years it was suggested that something approaching Formule Libre regulations were approved for the 1959 BRSCC series.

[As an aside, the author, a junior design engineer at Jaguar at the time, clearly recalls working on revised carburation/manifold arrangements for the 3.4s. Although most cars were supposedly 'private' entries, a number were provided with the latest kit by 'Lofty' England.]

As an example, this is what Jeff Uren (who would win the Championship in 1959) had to say about his Ford Zephyr: 'I told him [Ford's 'Edgy' Fabris] I'd win the 1959 Championship if he let me prepare the car at Lincoln Cars. I told Raymond Mays the same thing, if he would have BRM prepare my engines. Ray was fantastic – he built me two engines with the Mays head and triple Weber carbs (there was also a Servais straight-through exhaust system). And we did the chassis work at Lincoln Cars.

'By this time the car was quite special, the Mays cylinder head was aluminium, with a 10.0:1 compression ratio, and the 2.6-litre unit had a claimed power output of 168bhp at 5,800rpm. The suspension was lowered and stiffened – there were twin anti-roll bars at the front, for instance – and we also installed an anti-tramp bracket on the rear suspension, a super-quick (12.5:1) steering box, Girling disc brakes along with Michelin X radial tyres, lightweight bucket front seats and Perspex instead of glass in the side and rear windows.'

Thus equipped, the Zephyr was dominant in its 2.6-litre capacity class – for this eliminated the A105, whose 2,639cc engine was now too large! It was enough to give Uren the Championship, for although the Jaguar 3.4s invariably won individual races, too many of them – including Tommy Sopwith and Ivor Bueb – scrapped with each other, and none established a commanding class lead.

SUPATURAS – A DIVERSION

For 1960 the BRSCC then changed tack – or, rather, gave in to competitors who knew more about beating regulations than they did ! This time, therefore, they ran what they called the 'SupaTura' Championship (and, yes, that is the spelling they used), which was a 1-litre formula allowing any modifications that entrants could devise, except that the engine cylinder block had to be retained, and supercharging was banned. No larger-engined cars – no Zephyrs, no Jaguars, no Sunbeam Rapiers – could even compete.

For Ford, therefore, this was a season in which there was good news and bad news – the bad news was that Uren could not find time to defend his title; the good news was that John Young's Anglia 105E won two limited-capacity races outright, the first being a 1-litre race at Brands Hatch in May, a feat which he then repeated two months later on the same track.

This series comprised only six races. In the end it was 'Doc' Shepherd's amazing Austin A40 that proved so dominant in its class (he actually rolled it into a ball at the season-end race at Brands Hatch in October!). The A40 used engines prepared by Don Moore, with special head castings developed by Harry Weslake. For its day, 84bhp at 7,500rpm was an amazing power output for this engine – no wonder the car's top speed was more than 105mph!

Regrettably, the SupaTura regulations had not been a success in 1960 – competition was very thin at times, and 'Doc' Shepherd's A40 was quite outstanding – and a series of nods and winks from British car makers helped encourage another change. For 1961, therefore, the BRSCC changed its mind yet again, this time tightening up its regulations considerably, and decided that saloon cars should run to the still-modern Group 2 homologation rules. It was this format which would prevail from 1961 to 1965.

Although every race was invariably won by one or other of the Jaguar Mk II 3.8s (Tommy Sopwith's Equipe Endeavour cars were always competitive), relatively new models had more of a chance in smaller capacity classes – this being the period in which Borgward Isabellas (Bill Blydenstein), Sunbeam Rapiers (Peter Harper), and, of course, the fast-improving 850 Minis came to prominence.

The Easter Goodwood meeting was typical of what was to follow, with a line of Mk IIs leading the cavalcade (Mike Parkes, Graham Hill, Denis Taylor, Sir Gawaine Baillie and Bruce McLaren in that order) – and with Sir John Whitmore winning the 1,000cc class in his ex-works (rally team) Mini 850. As was now usual in this series, it was the car which was outstanding in its class that would win the Championship and, in spite of some spirited opposition from other Mini drivers such as Christabel Carlisle and Vic Elford, it was Sir John Whitmore who won the 'Mini class' so often.

If only we had known it, however, it was the appearance of Dan Gurney's huge 6.7-litre Chevrolet Impala at Silverstone in May which cast so many shadows over the future. Although this NASCAR-derived American car lost a wheel and had to retire, it led the race and set a new lap record. Many die-hards sniggered at the time, but the smiles would leave their faces in 1963 when the Sears/Ford Galaxie combination repeated the trick, with almost complete success.

From 1962, BMC decided that the new Mini-Cooper (the first of the 'homologation specials') was so promising in Group 2 form, that the BRSCC Championship was theirs for the taking. And so it was, but only in 1962, for Ford was just about to enter this sport in a big way. Even so, in 1962 one of several Jaguar Mk IIs was good enough to win every race, and it was John Love's 'works' Mini-Cooper, backed by Sir John Whitmore, which took 1.0-litre class honours, and the Trophy.

Then, as far as saloon car racing was concerned, 1963 saw a complete change around for the sport, as the Ford brand suddenly became prominent. In 1961 and 1962 no Ford had figured in the listings, but in 1963 there were Galaxies, Lotus-Cortinas and Cortina GTs in profusion.

For the first time an American car (the 450bhp/7.0-litre Galaxie) became a pace-setter – after which the Jaguars never again won a single race. Nor was that all. The first specially-developed Mini-Cooper S types appeared (originally with 1,071cc engines), and when the 1275S appeared in 1964 it would take 1.3-litre performance to a new level.

Two other new models also upset the status quo. First there was the Ford Cortina GT, which was soon followed by the twin-cam engined Lotus-Cortina (which had a twin-overhead-camshaft engine, sophisticated suspension, and was much lighter). Lotus-Cortinas with 160bhp (first homologated in September) instantly made cars like the Riley 1.5 and the Sunbeam Rapier obsolete, while a 1071S with 100bhp, disc brakes and front-wheel drive could make every other 1.3-litre car obsolete.

Because the Galaxie was American-derived (Holman & Moody had prepared it) and featured details such as a roll-cage (unheard of!), there was much trouble with scrutineers. Brakes (big drums, discs not being homologated until 1964) were a problem, as was adhesion on wet roads, but these cars won every race after their introduction in May.

Even so, it was the Lotus-Cortina (which gained homologation for the last two races of the season) that was much more promising. Those who

said that it could win races in 1964 were not disappointed. But it was the Galaxies that changed the face of saloon car racing, though no-one then realised that Mustangs and Falcons would challenge them in future.

By 1964, factory-backed Ford and BMC teams had virtually taken over from the private owners. Not only did F1 Champion Jim Clark's Lotus-Cortina dominate the series, but four of the top six in the standings, and two of the four class winners, were Fords. Except that Chris McLaren's Jaguar Mk II bravely won his (5-litre) capacity class on three occasions, and John Fitzpatrick showed just what an effective Mini-Cooper S driver he really was (the larger-engined 1275S was homologated before the season got properly under way), there were really few other talking points.

The real marker was laid down by the pace of Jim Clark's 160bhp Lotus-Cortina. Jim won three races outright, was second three times, and third in the other two races. He was demonstrably faster than any other Lotus-Cortina driver, on any surface, in any condition, anywhere. Yet in later years, an examination of his preserved/restored car showed that except for its engine a Lotus-Cortina was still a very simple machine.

Jim, on the other hand, was not – and somehow he found time from his F1 commitments with Lotus, to tackle every one of the races, at Snetterton, Goodwood, Oulton Park, Aintree, Silverstone, Crystal Palace and Brands Hatch. The only times that he was ever beaten was by one of the 7.0-litre Galaxies (which now ran with front disc brakes).

This was a season-long astonishing demonstration of Jim's abilities – for he always seemed to have his car on three wheels longer and higher than any of his team-mates and rivals. One first-corner shot which I have seen, of the Gold Cup meeting at Oulton Park, shows Jack Sears' Galaxie leading five Lotus-Cortinas, a Jaguar, four Mini-Cooper Ss, another Galaxie and two Anglia 1200s.

Certain trends were obvious – and the first rumblings, which led to a major change in regulations at the end of the following (1965) season, began. Within two years, it seemed, saloon cars specially developed for motorsport had come on apace, and if a manufacturer needed to sell a limited number for normal road-car use, so be it. Without success in motorsport as the aim, the Mini-Cooper S and the Lotus-Cortina would never have been developed, and seriously professional 'works' teams such as the Cooper Car Co. and Team Lotus would not have evolved.

Accordingly, and with the exception of beautifully-prepared Ford Mustangs (Roy Pierpoint won the Championship in one of them, though Alan Mann Racing built the car) it was those professional teams that really ruled the roost. Not only were Lotus-Cortinas just as good as expected (though Jim Clark could not compete in all the events), but in their 1.3-litre class a number of Mini-Cooper 1275Ss squabbled for victory. Lessons learned were that big V8-engined American cars could now guarantee to win most of the races, and that there was really no way that ordinary saloons could hope to beat specially-developed and specially-homologated cars.

The teams realised this, the BRSCC realised this and – most important – the spectators realised this. Unless terminal boredom was to set in, more variety was needed. For 1966 therefore, it seemed, the solution was to adopt Group 5 regulations.

Mike Hawthorn's Jaguar 3.4, on its way to winning the saloon car race at Silverstone in 1958, after a stirring battle with Tommy Sopwith's 3.4, which he eventually won by 0.6 seconds. Incidentally, this was Mike's own road car, which he drove back to Farnham at the end of the day!

↑ In 1958, at the British GP support race at Silverstone, Tommy Sopwith led the race for some time, until his Jaguar 3.4 suddenly shed a rear wheel at Becketts Corner and ground to a halt. In his place, American Walt Hansgen then took the usual Jaguar victory.

→ In the first year of the BRSCC Championship, Jack Sears (Austin A105) and Jeff Uren (Ford Zephyr) usually raced together as close as this. First Sears led...

↓ ...then Uren led. Both these pictures were taken in the same event, at Silverstone.

↑ Jeff Uren won the BRSCC Championship in 1959, in his Ford Zephyr Mk II. Here he is at Brands Hatch, receiving the Championship trophy, from BMC Competitions Manager Marcus Chambers.

↖ Racing variety in the 1958 BRSCC, with David Haynes' Ford Zephyr Mk II ahead of two Austin A35s, an MG Magnette ZA, a Fiat 1100TV and a Borgward Isabella.

← It didn't matter which circuit was in use – this was Goodwood in 1959 – Jaguars were invariably in front in the late 1950s. Both cars are 3.4s, with Ivor Bueb leading Roy Salvadori.

➡ Masses of power and lots of rubber being laid at the start of the British GP support race at Aintree in July 1962. Bob Janes of Australia would lead the race in the white Coombs car, but crash later, while Jack Sears, on the camera-left of this front-row shot, would win the race.

↑ 'Listen very carefully, I shall say this only once...' – team manager Ken Tyrrell explaining the tactics to his Mini-Cooper racers in 1962. John Whitmore is in the centre of the frame, while John Love (left) has clearly heard it all before.

↖ Where the regulations favoured outstanding cars in their class, the Minis invariably came out on top. Sir John Whitmore, driving an 850 Mini, won the Championship in 1961. This is Oulton Park and the Gold Cup meeting.

↙ Sunbeam was serious about saloon car racing until its Rapiers (these were 'works' rally cars stripped out for circuit racing) were overwhelmed by lighter, more modern, opposition. Here is Peter Harper ahead of Paddy Hopkirk's 997cc-engined Mini-Cooper.

Team-mates or rivals? Two 'works' Rapiers in wheel-to-wheel action in 1960 with Peter Harper (closest to the camera) and Keith Ballisat at the wheels.

In 1962 and 1963 Christabel Carlisle was one of the fastest and most accomplished Mini-Cooper racers. Love that personalised registration number.

Before the age of homologation specials matured, some of the strangest cars were entered in British saloon car races: this was the end-of-season 6-Hour race at Brands Hatch, with the Uren/Haynes Zodiac Mk III ahead of the Foster/Hedges MG100.

⬆ The monstrous Ford Galaxie, seen here at Crystal Palace with Jack Sears driving it, changed the face of British saloon car racing at a stroke. Before the Galaxie appeared, Jaguar always won, but after it settled into British racing, Jaguar never won another race.

↗ By 1963 the Old Order was changing rapidly. Here at Brands Hatch, a 3.8-litre Mk II Jaguar is being harassed by one of the Willment Cortina GTs. Once the more powerful Lotus-Cortinas were homologated, it really was 'Game Over'.

➡ The Willment Cortina GTs were not only fast but light and nimble. Jack Sears used one early in 1963, before his 7-litre Galaxie arrived, and proved that this was a quicker car than Alan Hutcheson's smaller Riley 1.5.

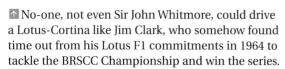
No-one, not even Sir John Whitmore, could drive a Lotus-Cortina like Jim Clark, who somehow found time out from his Lotus F1 commitments in 1964 to tackle the BRSCC Championship and win the series.

→ Snetterton in 1963, where the front row of the BRSCC race grid was contested by two 7.0-litre Galaxies, Jim Clark's 'works' 1.6-litre Lotus-Cortina, and a Jaguar 3.8 Mk II. The Old Order Changeth.

Three different Mini-Cooper 1275Ss at Oulton Park, with a private owner temporarily leading Warwick Banks's 'works' car and John Handley's Broadspeed car bringing up the rear. The Broadspeed cars sometimes beat the 'works' cars – which was not what the Abingdon Game Plan wanted to see.

↑ Colourful line-up at the start of the Silverstone race of May 1965, with two of the ex-Alan Mann Tour de France Mustangs sharing the front-row of the grid with the 'works' Lotus-Cortinas. Roy Pierpoint (Comp. No. 42) won the race, with Sir Gawaine Baillie (No. 40) second.

← BJH 418B was the sister car to Jim Clark's Championship winning car in 1964, and was usually driven by Pete Arundell. This was Silverstone.

At the end of the Group 2 era in 1965, competition in Britain and in Europe was always close – in this case one of the Alan Mann Lotus-Cortinas being neck-and-neck with a 4.2-litre Ford Mustang.

The Lotus-Cortina race cars prepared by Team Lotus always seemed to cock an inside front wheel on sweeping corners, like this, but drivers like Jim Clark came to love the handling balance which resulted from it. From 1963 to 1965 the Lotus-Cortinas set every standard, after which the rules changed and the Group 5 Falcons took over.

↑ In the last year of Group 2 racing – 1965 – American Fords dominated the saloon car races. This was the famous chicane at Goodwood, with one of the enormously effective 7.0-litre Galaxies about to swallow up Ted Savory's bright yellow Mustang.

↖ In 1962, although Christabel Carlisle's 997cc engined Mini-Cooper looked modest enough, engine tuner Don Moore made sure that it was one of the fastest of all the Minis in this period.

← No sooner had BMC developed the Mini-Cooper S, and got it homologated, it became a leading 'class' car in the British Saloon Car Championship. This was the modest little Cooper Car Co. set up of 1963, as seen at Silverstone.

⬆ Roy Pierpoint's 4.2-Litre Mustang won the 1965 Championship, but that would be a one-off success, as when Group 5 regulations were adopted for 1966, it was overwhelmed by the faster and more powerful Falcons.

⬅ Telling tales out of school? Left to right: Jack Sears, Sir John Whitmore, Jochen Neerpasch (of Ford-Germany) and Tommy Sopwith.

1966–1969

When the BRSCC changed its Saloon Car Championship regulations for the 1966 season – from Group 2 to Group 5 – this allowed more technical freedom to the entrants, and helped make many manufacturers' cars instantly competitive.

Under Group 5 rules, except for the compulsion of retaining the standard engine cylinder block and the same basic body structure, engineers were allowed to change almost everything else.

There was freedom of choice on brakes, engine tuning (though the original camshaft position and block casting had to be retained), transmissions (within the same casing), ultra-wide (non-homologated) wheels, and lightened body and 'glass' panels. Although cars used had to be genuine mass-production machines, and had to be homologated into Group 2, car manufacturers no longer had to build a minimum number of them as 'homologation specials' so that their race cars might become competitive. This meant that mundane cars like the Ford Anglia 105E and the Hillman Imp, previously quite outstripped (when running in homologated guise) by the Mini-Cooper S, could get back on terms.

Not only that, but it made it possible for American cars other than the gargantuan Ford Galaxies and Mustangs to be competitive. In particular, the ever-resourceful Alan Mann discovered a way of using up the fleet of 4.7-litre Ford Falcons which had originally been built as Group 2 cars for the 1964 Monte Carlo rally, and which had languished thereafter. What happened was an object lesson in how to make the very most of Group 5 regulations.

By the end of the 1964 rally season, several tired old Falcons were in store in AMR's Byfleet premises, with no further motorsport programmes in mind, and not seeming to be suitable for any other type of sport. For 1966 however, several of these cars were redeveloped, found to weigh 400lb/181kg less than the equivalent Mustang, fitted with much wider (8.5in/216mm wide) wheel rims, and modified rear suspensions, which encompassed coil springs and radius arms.

Suddenly, these became formidable-looking racers. By the end of 1966, the Falcons had won three races, and took another five podium positions, and would go on to improve in future years. Alan Mann would dig out yet another Falcon for Frank Gardner to drive in 1967, when he won the Championship outright. By this time four-wheel disc brakes and a full 5-litre V8 engine had been adopted, and with 400bhp this was a sure-fire winner.

The usual class structure, and class point-scoring structure, was retained for 1966, and it wasn't long before each was dominated by a particular car. V8-engined American 'Formula Ford' monsters – Falcons, Mustangs and Galaxies – often won outright, 'works' Lotus-Cortinas from Team Lotus always won the 2-litre category (F1 hero Jim Clark won three races and two classes, Jacky Ickx and Peter Arundell several others), 1.3-litre Superspeed Anglias (Mike Young and Chris Craft) won nine times, while John Fitzpatrick blitzed the 1-litre category in his superbly-engineered Broadspeed Anglia.

In some cases, though, it was going to take time for all competing cars to reach the same white-hot level of competitiveness. At this stage neither the 'works' BMC Mini-Cooper S (which didn't start using eight-port cylinder heads until late in the season), nor the 1.0-litre 'works' Rallye Imps (run by Rootes dealer Alan Fraser) had the pace before the end of the year, though for 1967 they had plans. Not only that, but there were threats of a Porsche presence for 1967 too...

For the spectators this was all stirring stuff, for all the cars were clearly going, handling and stopping as never before. The most powerful cars (all American Fords) had at least 400bhp, the Lotus-Cortinas pushed out 180bhp, and even the Broadspeed Anglias churned out 115bhp at a screaming 9,200rpm.

There was an upside – and a simultaneous downside. Fuel injection, five-speed gearboxes inside standard four-speed casings, limited-slip differentials, magnesium wheels and completely re-engineered suspensions were all found, on all competitive cars – and at every meeting the cars seemed to get quicker. The downside was that they became demonstrably more costly and special, but the teams tried to shrug this off. Even so, after only one season the RAC MSA must have realised that they had a technological tiger by its tail.

A complex points scoring system saw John Fitzpatrick's Broadspeed Anglia narrowly beating John Rhodes' BMC Mini-Cooper S to the drivers' title, while Team Lotus won the Entrants' Championship, for consistency was more important than individual brilliance.

The second Group 5 season was even more exciting than the first, not only because all the established cars (particularly the V8-engined Fords, and the Lotus-Cortinas) were more powerful than before, but because each of the smaller-engined cars was developed to a new peak of power and performance. The combination of newly rebuilt Ford Falcon (400 muscley horsepower) in flamboyant red-and-gold livery, expert preparation by Alan Mann Racing, and ruthlessly-effective driving by Frank Gardner produced seven outright victories, and Championship victory at a canter.

Not only did existing teams improve the cars which had performed so well in 1966 – the 1.0-litre Broadspeed Anglias had fuel injection and 124bhp, 'works' Mini-Cooper Ss had eight-port heads and John Rhodes' inimitable driving skills, and Team Lotus Mk 2 Lotus-Cortinas appeared with 205bhp Ford-Cosworth FVA F2 engines (amazingly, the regulations seemed to allow this for alternative cylinder heads were allowed at the time and the original camshaft position was retained – though there were now two atop the engine – and this was a Cortina-based engine, although several eyebrows were raised when they first appeared). By now fully-developed, the Fraser Imps were race-competitive (with fuel injection and 115bhp), so with Vic Elford's Porsche 911 (don't ask how, but it had somehow been homologated as a Group 2 car!) also fighting it out with the Lotus-Cortinas, this was another exciting season.

It was more and more obvious, however, that under Group 5 regulations, victory in the Touring Car Championship would inevitably go to the team that could spend the most time, effort and finance in cruising up to the limit of the regulations, and reworking cars to their own advantage. All very exciting for the spectators, and the media, but increasingly predictable: knowing what cars were available at the start of a season, it was becoming possible to forecast winners for the end of that season!

In normal weather conditions, it now seemed inevitable that victory in individual races would go to one or other of the ex-Monte Falcons. In 1967, if Gardner's AMR car did not win, Sir Gawaine Baillie or Roy Pierpoint in sister Falcons might do the job instead or, failing that, F1 driver Jackie Oliver in a Mustang. The truly startling battles were in the smaller-capacity classes, where Mini-Cooper S fought against 1.3-litre Anglia, or Hillman Rallye Imp against 1.0-litre Anglia.

It was close, but not that close, for Gardner finished comfortably at the top of the standings, and on this occasion Fitzpatrick (Anglia) beat John Rhodes (Mini-Cooper S), on points though in a different capacity class, by a small but significant margin.

It was at this point that the most important single development, to date, in the development of the British Touring Car racing arrived. In January 1968 Ford announced a new range of Escorts – of which the flagship was the Twin-Cam. Then, as in later years with the Sierra RS500 Cosworth, Ford recognised the need to build a proper 'homologation special' for motor sport. Although it was an all-can-do competition car, the Twin-Cam was an ideal Group 2 base from which to evolve a white-hot, dominant, Group 5 machine.

Forty years on, a Twin-Cam looks quite ordinary today, and feels quite sedate, but in 1968 the implications of a compact twin-cam engined saloon were enormous. Think of a Lotus-Cortina whose body shell had been shrink-wrapped around the same running gear, and from which much weight had been cut away. That was what the Twin-Cam was all about, and it showed every sign of revolutionising the Touring Car scene.

Because it could not be homologated until May 1968 (and even then, Ford had to tell a few white lies to get it accepted as being genuinely 'in production' at that time), the opposition at least had some time to garner a few victories, but after that there was no hiding place.

Not only did the Twin-Cam excel – even as a 1.6-litre, it won two races outright in 1968, and always led its class – but its 'little brother' the Broadspeed-prepared Escort 1300GT (which took time to become reliable), raised standards at every circuit, in all conditions. Because the now ageing Falcons (the same old cars as in 1964, but progressively rebuilt, modernised and further developed) won no fewer than nine of the eleven races, this really was 'Formula Ford' at its most crushing. Not that it was totally one-sided in Championship terms, for BMC, whose Mini-Coopers had won this Championship in 1962, were still trying to improve the 1275S, which allowed John Rhodes' (in an eight-port headed car) to take three class victories and a string of consistent finishes throughout the year.

Although their season had started unhappily, with FVA-engined Lotus-Cortinas, the revelation of the year was the standard of preparation, and the technical sophistication, of the new Alan Mann Racing Escort Twin-Cam, and the driving of that gritty Aussie Frank Gardner. Powered by 1.6-litre Cosworth-Ford FVA (F2) engines, and with 205bhp, this machine was a big step ahead of any other 1.6-litre car, and was never beaten in eight races. It was so outstanding that, on its own, it led to the RAC deciding to ban the use of alternative cylinder heads in 1969! The second AMR Escort, incidentally, turned out with a 'supercharged' eight-valve twin-cam engine – which meant that an electric fan motor blew air into the intake trumpets, merely to allow the car to run in the over 2-litre category! It was not a success.

Even so, except for the two events won outright by the AMR Escort (both times at Brands Hatch), every race was won by one of several Falcons. Brian Muir's car won six races (the first five races, on the trot, one of them using a supercharged 5.3-litre version of the big V8 engine!), Roy Pierpoint won one, and David Hobbs one. Neither Mustangs nor Galaxies figured any more, and no other competitive American machine had yet been completed. The Falcons were big, fast, flamboyant and amazingly nimble. When crashes occurred, showers of fibre-glass would remind us all of their very special character, but they seemed to be quick to repair – and on every occasion they appeared to be fully competitive.

This was Group 5 racing at its fastest and most expensive best. Although Ford seemed to have the outright victories sewn up, other cars – notably the 'works' Minis and the 'works-backed' Broadspeed Escorts – brought real life to the smaller capacity classes. The pity of it all was that Chrysler (which now controlled the Rootes Group) had withdrawn support from the Fraser Imps, which rarely appeared, while the Porsche 911s which ought to have fought head-to-head against Gardner in the 2-litre category rarely turned out either.

Even before the 1969 season began, the RAC MSA had banned the use of alternative cylinder heads unless they were already homologated. This meant that FVA-engined Escorts or Lotus-Cortinas could no longer go racing, though the eight-port BMC Mini-Cooper Ss were still eligible. Soon, too, rumours began to spread, that this might be a final fling for the Group 5 category cars. For 1970, it was said, the RAC had already decided to drop the Group 5 formula, in favour of Group 2. This, it was thought, would not only bring car specifications some way back towards being 'normal', and recognisable to the track-side spectators, but they might even bring down costs too.

Accordingly, there were few mechanical innovations to be ushered in, and refined, for 1969 – though Roy Pierpoint's shapely Chevrolet Camaro was a novelty from mid-season, and Equipe Arden's Mini-Cooper S proved that, once and for all, the combination of a tiny high-revving (970S) engine and a nimble chassis was still impressive. The end-of-season Championship table, though, tells its own story for no fewer than 13 of the top 20 finishers' cars carried Ford badges, five others being one or other BMC Mini-Cooper Ss.

Although it was the Big Bangers, winning races, that made all the immediate headlines, it was the sheer consistency of class contenders that garnered Championship points. Roy Pierpoint won six of the twelve races (four times in his faithful Falcon, then twice in a 5.0-litre Chevrolet Camaro), but it was Chris Craft (Broadspeed Escort GT – six class victories) and Alec Poole (seven class wins in the privately-prepared Mini-Cooper 970S) who built up more points. Although there was a fleet of Escort Twin-Cams in the 2-litre class, no one driver dominated the standings, so Mike Crabtree won it, though Rod Mansfield, John Hine and Barry Pearson were all competitive.

↑ After British Leyland had ditched their contract, in 1969 the John Cooper team joined forces with Britax and Downton to race these bright yellow Group 5 Mini-Cooper 1275Ss.

↖ When the BTCC embraced Group 5 regulations, the ex-Monte Carlo Rally Ford Falcons soon proved to be regular race winners. This was Goodwood in 1966, where one of the cars has nibbled away at the glass-fibre front wing – a regular 'war wound' of these big cars.

← Under Group 5 regulations, Mustangs like this machine could be competitive, but as they weighed a lot more than the Falcons they did not make as many race wins.

⬆ In the Group 5 era, large could usually beat small – but not by much. One of the ex-Monte Carlo Rally Falcons leading Frank Gardner's famous Escort Twin-Cam on Paddock Hill Bend at Brands Hatch in 1968.

↗ In the Group 5 era of the late 1960s, there was great racing, but little glitz. This was a paddock scene, of the two 'works' Mini-Cooper 1275S cars which made 1.3-litre racing so exciting. Note the 'T Car', the spare also used for practice.

➡ In 1966 the 'works' Group 5 Lotus-Cortinas were more sophisticated than ever before, with a modified type of wishbone front suspension, and fuel-injected twin-cam engines. Peter Arundell finished third overall in the Championship.

⬆ In 1966 Ralph Broad, leaning in to the car, took up a Ford contract for the Group 5 period, preparing astonishingly fast 1-litre Anglia 105Es. Anita Taylor, here taking instructions, was one of Ralph's star drivers.

↗ Showroom-specification Ford Anglias never looked like this – for this was a 135bhp Group 5 version of the 1.3-litre engine, as prepared by Superspeed.

➡ In 1966 and 1967 the Broadspeed Anglias were much the fastest 1-litre machines. Not only did they have a lot of horsepower – 115bhp at least – but drivers like John Fitzpatrick and (here) Anita Taylor loved the way these immaculate cars always handled.

From 1968 Broadspeed moved up to running a brace of 145bhp/1.3-litre engined Ford Escort GTs, with two drivers (Chris Craft ahead, John Fitzpatrick right behind him) who often finished nose to tail.

Chris Craft (Superspeed Anglia Super) ahead of John Rhodes' 'works' Mini-Cooper 1275S at Oulton Park in 1966. Small-capacity racing was always close at this time.

⮕ One of the smart maroon Broadspeed Escort 1300GTs in full cry at Brands Hatch in 1969. By this time these Escorts were invincible in their class.

⬇ With Frank Gardner as their driver, and the newly-homologated Escort Twin-Cam as their Group 5 tool, Alan Mann Racing set out to win the 1968 Championship (which they did). Gardner did not win many races, but was invincible in his class, for the regulations allowed him to use a 16-valve Cosworth FVA F2 engine up front! Looking as good as it always did, XOO 349F survives to this day.

⬆Alan Mann, the quiet team manager with a huge reputation. Throughout the 1960s his cars – Fords of one model or another – won hundreds of races in the UK and in Europe. Not only did he prepare Lotus-Cortinas and Escorts for racing, but Falcons for the Monte Carlo Rally, and Mustangs for the Tour de France. – all of which were winning machines.

⬈In 1968 and 1969, the battle for Group 5 supremacy was usually between one of Alan Mann Racing's Escort Twin-Cams, and one of several glass-fibre panelled Ford Falcons.

➡ In 1968 and 1969 the Broadspeed Escort GTs were usually supreme in the 1.3-litre category. This was John Fitzpatrick at Silverstone.

Vic Elford (or 'Quick Vic' as he was nicknamed), joined Porsche in 1967. In the next few years he would win in races and rallies, in Britain, Europe and North America, while in 1967 he raced this ex-AFN demonstrator, GVB 911D, as a Group 5 machine in the British Championship. By no means as specialised as the Ford competition, it sometimes beat them – but the racing was always close.

Early in 1968 Frank Gardner was awaiting the homologation of the new Escort Twin-Cam, so used this Alan Mann racing-prepared/FVA-engined Lotus-Cortina instead. The colour scheme was familiar, but this car was not as nimble as the Escort that would follow. This was Brands Hatch in March 1968.

With Ford's love affair with saloon car racing at its height, they attracted many famous names to race their cars. This was the Belgian, Lucien Bianchi, at Silverstone in 1967.

⬅ Frank Gardner of Australia, tall, lanky, laconic and likely to floor any interviewer with his one-liner repartee, was one of Britain's most successful racers, and in this FVA-engined Escort he enjoyed formidable success.

⬆ This was Frank Gardner in his 'other Escort' (if, that is, we can trust registration numbers) at Mallory Park in the summer of 1968. There's no other car in sight because Gardner has already outstripped his opposition.

⬆CTC 24E was one of the Team Lotus Lotus-Cortina Mk II team cars of 1967, which had a tough time battling against the much more powerful Falcons of the period. Paul Hawkins was giving it his all at Silverstone.

◥Gardner at Bottom Bend at Brands Hatch in 1968, almost a home-from-home for this red-and-gold AMR Twin-Cam in 1968.

◤Group 5 variety in 1967 with Vic Elford's Porsche 911 just rushing out of shot, closely harried by a 'works' Lotus-Cortina Mk II, and a 1966 model right behind that.

↑ Although the ubiquitous Minis could not be tuned as much as the Ford Anglias and Escorts, they still went round corners faster than any other machine! This was John Rhodes in one of the 1969 cars, which were prepared at Abingdon.

↗ Frank Gardner's four-year-old glass-fibre winged Ford Falcon won the 1967 Championship with the greatest of ease – in that year alone it won seven races in all.

→ As prepared by Alan Mann Racing for 1967, this was the fastest and most consistently successful of all the 1964-vintage Ford Falcons, which quite dominated Group 5 racing towards the end of the 1960s. Much lighter than they looked, the 4.7-litre (sometimes even 5.0-litre) engined cars were monstrously powerful, and remarkably nimble too.

⬆ Superspeed built several extremely fast and powerful 1.3-litre Anglia 105Es in 1966 and 1967, these often having the beating of the 'works' Mini-Cooper Ss. This was Mike Young, one of the brothers who ran Superspeed.

◤ Group 5 regulations allowed resourceful tuners to transform a very basic car into a real racer. A 'showroom' Ford Anglia Super like this probably had 48bhp, but Superspeed could extract over 135bhp while still remaining inside the regulations!

◁ In the late 1960s, if the weather was good, an Anglia like this Superspeed example was usually competitive with the Mini-Cooper 1275S – but if it rained, the front-wheel-drive Minis then left the conventional Ford for dead.

For three seasons in the Group 5 era, when there was a 1-litre class, Hillman Imps prepared by Alan Fraser's Rootes dealership were often close to the performance of the Broadspeed Anglias. The Coventry-Climax-based engine was extremely tuneable, and drivers like Bernard Unett (seen here at Brands Hatch) made the most of the rear-engined car's agility too.

Roy Pierpoint's glass-fibre winged Falcon was one of the most successful of all Group 5 cars in the late 1960s, but often lost bits of the shell (like the front bumper on this occasion) in close racing at the front.

Early in 1968 Frank Gardner raced not one but two different Lotus-Cortina Mk IIs, both of which used the same precious 1.6-litre/220bhp Cosworth FVA F2 engine – an engine that would finally be bequeathed to the Escort Twin-Cam which he would eventually race later in the year.

Group 5 racing could be incredibly close, particularly at class level towards the middle of the field. Here at Silverstone in 1967 is a tight group including a Superspeed Anglia (1.3-litres), a 'works' Mini-Cooper S (1.3-litres) and a Broadspeed Anglia (1.0-litre). Who knows how the order would change by the time they reached the next corner!

Forty years on, but this Goodwood Revival shot gives a perfect idea of the variety of cars seen in Group 5 racing in the 1960s. Mustang, Galaxie, Falcon, Lotus-Cortina and Jaguar Mk II are all in the front lines, with Minis, Fords and other Jaguars all following up. This was an exciting time to go motor racing, and the Revival Meeting makes sure we all remember that.

After British Leyland dumped the Cooper race team, the 'works' rally team at Abingdon produced its own Mini racers for 1969. This was John Handley's car, carrying the identity of an old rally car!

Goodwood, the Revival Meeting of 2005, but in an atmosphere which is absolutely redolent of Group 5 racing at its best. A Galaxie, Mini-Cooper S, and two Falcons are in the front row, with Jaguar, Lotus-Cortina and BMW right behind.

⬆ This is why the spectators found Group 5 racing so exciting in 1968. Soon after the start of this Brands Hatch race, two of the ubiquitous Falcons and both the Alan Mann Racing Escort Twin-Cams scrabble around Paddock Hill Bend, with Lotus-Cortinas, Escorts and the rest of the field close behind.

◥ Power, real power, on the front row of the grid at Silverstone in July 1968. No fewer than three of the lightweight Falcons loom over Frank Gardner's Escort Twin-Cam. The Escort would win the race outright, with guest-star Hubert Hahne second in one of those 4.7-litre Falcons.

◄ Competition between the Mini-Cooper Ss and Escort GTs was always incredibly close in 1968 – Paddock Hill Bend at Brands Hatch.

In 1967 Frank Gardner was almost unbeatable in the familiar red/gold colours of Alan Mann's highly-developed Falcon, and won the Championship quite comfortably.

1970–1973

If anyone following the British Saloon Car Championship had expected speeds to fall after the changeover from Group 5 to Group 2, they were speedily proved wrong. In 1970, in fact, the new breed of Group 2 cars broke lap records at almost every circuit, in every capacity class. The RAC MSA, for sure, was somewhat taken aback by this – especially as this was merely at the start of a four-year life of Group 2 competition.

And if the same administrators had been hoping for more varied results, they were proved wrong there too. Even so, they only needed to look at the roughly parallel sport of world-level rallying to see what might happen. Big companies with big ambitions, and the marketing intention to back up their dreams, could always meet a new challenge in the regulations. Ford, in particular, was about to homologate the sport's first 16-valve engine in the Escort RS1600, which would start racing in 1970/71, and soon produce previously unheard of amounts of power. To quote Quentin Spurring's Seasonal Survey of the 1970 season in *Autosport*, '...the racing in Britain was on the whole disappointing. This was not so much because they were processional – with four classes in each event they could hardly be that – but because the results became extremely predictable. Frank Gardner (Boss Mustang), Chris Craft (Escort Twin Cam), John Fitzpatrick (Escort GT) and Bill McGovern (Sunbeam Imp) were far superior to their class rivals, and certain to win unless mechanical or other troubles intervened...'

If there was a change of cars and faces in the winning circles it was because fashions, rather than draconian rules, had changed. At the front, the 'Detroit Iron' mainly comprised modern Mustangs and Camaros, Escorts of one type or another were everywhere in the middle of the field, and because the Minis had been rendered impotent by the change to Group 2 they were nowhere to be found. One statistic tells its own story – of 44 drivers scoring Championship points in 1970, 20 of them were in Ford-badged machinery. At the 'heavy-metal' end, eight cars came from Detroit.

Number-crunchers will want to know that Frank Gardner's car won eight of eleven races with his 420bhp Mustang, Chris Craft won six classes with his 177bhp Broadspeed Escort Twin-Cam, Fitzpatrick's Broadspeed 149bhp Escort GT won seven times, but it was Bill McGovern in a new Sunbeam-badged Rallye Imp, who was even more consistent, winning eight classes and finishing second twice. The Imp was owned and prepared by George Bevan, who described himself as a 'kitchen utensil manufacturer', and had a 108bhp engine with camshaft by Piper, who were real experts at this sort of thing – it was badged 'Sunbeam' rather than 'Hillman', incidentally, because it was that brand which received most of the new homologation pieces developed by Chrysler's Des O'Dell during the year!

Even though Frank Gardner's Boss Mustang was much the most accomplished of all the 'Detroit Iron', all of them were thunderously fast in a straight line, of course, and the start and early-lap spectacles were just as exciting as they had been at the height of the Falcon/Mustang boom of the late 1960s.

Yet the rest of the racing was, somehow, rather dull, and little changed in 1971 to brighten things up much more. Although Brian Muir won seven races in Chevrolet Camaros (the first sponsored by Wiggins Teape, the second by SCA Freight too), and apart from a couple of victories for Gerry Birrell in a genuine 'works' Ford Capri RS2600 from Cologne, the main talking points, as ever, were among the smaller cars and classes.

With the Escort RS1600 finally homologated, in 1971 it was Broadspeed that made headlines, building a new Ford, with the latest Lucas-injected 240bhp/1.7-litre BDA engine. As in 1970, its rear suspension featured Watts linkage, and there were huge F1-size disc brakes. All this, allied to determined driving by John Fitzpatrick, produced a car that dominated its class and challenged for outright victories.

For this particular car/team/driver combination, it was an eventful season. Having won outright at Brands Hatch, then coming second at Snetterton, it was then destroyed at Thruxton after a front stub axle breakage. A completely re-shelled car then took a series of second, third and fourth places during the year, before once again winning outright at Brands Hatch in September.

Then came the final race of the season, at Brands Hatch, where Fitzpatrick's RS1600 battled for the lead with Frank Gardner's Camaro, the cars banging repeatedly into each other. The big Camaro suffered a catastrophic tyre explosion, veered into the Escort, nudged it into multiple rolls and wrote it off – for the second time in a season! After this, it was really no consolation to know that Fitzpatrick had won the 2-litre class in the series.

Pyrotechnics apart, it is a measure of the 1971 season that no fewer than 25 of the 44 drivers who scored points were driving Fords of one sort or another – 22 of these being Escort GTs, Twin-Cams or RS1600s. Seven of the eight cars to figure in the 1-litre class, which Bill McGovern's 112bhp car almost invariably won, were Imps, and all but one car in the 2-litre category was an Escort Twin-Cam or RS1600. Yet even though the most powerful of the Camaros and Mustangs were reputedly pushing out 500bhp (from a push-rod 5-litre V8 engine!) the racing was not as exuberant as it had been in the late 1960s.

Except for one startling development – the performance of Jonathan Buncombe's Richard Longman-prepared Mini-Cooper 1275S (which won the 1.3-litre category ahead of Vince Woodman's Escort 1300GT) – 1972 was almost a rerun of 1971, which led some cynics to start muttering 'boring, boring...' at the results. The fact is that Frank Gardner's SCA Freight Chevrolet Camaro almost invariably won the races, while Dave Matthews (1.8-litre RS1600), Vince Woodman (unless thwarted by mechanical ill luck) and Bill McGovern (Sunbeam Rallye Imp) won the classes.

As ever, it was patient points accumulation in the classes, rather than outright victories, that counted for everything in the RAC series, and since McGovern was a dedicated expert at that strategy by this time, he not only won his class, but the Championship outright – for the third consecutive season. Interestingly enough, no sooner did the RAC announce a change in Championship regulations for 1974 (when Group 1 would replace Group 2), than McGovern and the Imps disappeared from the Championship scene. Because it was an ageing model (and not one that was making any money for the company) McGovern's car had not been supported from the Chrysler factory, and except for a celebratory lunch in the Engineering HQ in Coventry (which the author attended) there was little recognition of his performances.

In almost all respects, therefore, the 1972 season was indeed a rerun of 1971 – the only major developments being that Brian Muir's Gartlan-prepared Ford Capri RS2600 occasionally gave Gardner's Camaro a fright, and Dave Matthews took over from John Fitzpatrick as the outstanding Escort RS1600 pilot. Muir's Capri sometimes proved to be unreliable, but was definitely superior in the wet, while Matthews was often harried by Dave Brodie's RS1600, which was also not as reliable.

At all levels, the cars were now astonishingly capable, their pace making Group 5 of the 1960s look like a different era, which it truly was. When one considered that tyre technology continued to increase in leaps and bounds, that cars like Gardner's 5.7-litre Chevrolet had up to 500bhp, and that even 1.3-litre Escorts like that of Vince Woodman had up to 150bhp, it was not at all surprising. Yet for the spectators, there were few novelties, and with race results being somewhat predictable their interest sagged a little.

The support race to the British GP meeting at Brands Hatch was a case in point. Muir's Capri led Gardner from the start, then missed a gear and spun off on a patch of oil, after which the Camaro won at a canter. Gardner averaged no less than 92.65mph on the full GP circuit (this compared with Emerson Fittipaldi's F1-winning pace of 112.06mph) and four of the next five finishers were in Escort RS1600s, the fastest of which was Dave Brodie's car. *Autocar*'s Ray Hutton then summed up everything by writing that: '...the smallest category was, as usual, an easy victory for Championship leader Bill McGovern in George Bevan's Imp...'

Something had to be done to perk up some more interest for 1973 – especially because the RAC, the circuit owners and Championship promoters had all reacted to the public mood. A subsidiary championship, promoted at other events, had already established a Group 1 series, which seemed to be very popular and very competitive. Accordingly, the RAC decided to impose Group 1 regulations for the Saloon Car Championship in 1974. It was well that they did, for after that decision had been made, the Middle East war erupted, oil supply embargoes were swiftly applied by OPEC (the Organisation of Petroleum Exporting Countries), and a full-scale energy/oil supply crisis developed.

In 1973, therefore, we saw the last of the truly ultra-powered saloon car races (until 1987, that is, when Ford's mighty Sierra RS500 Cosworth appeared), and all the competitive cars were more sophisticated and more powerful than ever. Not only did Frank Gardner's SCA Freight-sponsored Camaro have an amazing 7.0-litre V8 engine, but several ultra-competitive Escort RS1600s were fitted with 260/270bhp alloy-blocked 2-litre engines – while Ford also astonished everyone by homologating a new engine derivative for the Escort 1300GT (a 1.3-litre version of the 16-valve BDA engine, the BDH, this being so efficient that it produced up to 190bhp). Only a year earlier we had all been impressed by Broadspeed's 150bhp from push-rod power, but this 16-valve screamer put everything else into the shade.

Even though this was very much 'Formula Gardner' in 1973 (Robert Fearnall, writing in *Autosport*, stated that: 'The spectators loved the sight of Gardner in the thundering Camaro, usually being chased by Brian Muir's BMW [3.0CSL] with its wonderful singing high-pitched shrill...'), there was great interest in the smaller capacity classes.

This was the season in which Dave Matthews moved up, from a 1.3-litre car, by running a new 2-litre alloy-blocked Escort RS1600, which had been prepared by Ford Motorsport at Boreham; Andy Rouse (who had won the Ford Mexico Series one-make Championship in 1972), started racing 'real' Escorts for Broadspeed; and Dave Brodie's immaculate Escort was equally as fast as anything developed by the Ford factory.

Even so, this was a season in which spectator and competitor interest in the Saloon Car Championship sagged badly. Although the season was dominated by Frank Gardner's massive-engined Chevrolet Camaro (with Brian Muir's BMW 3.0CSL offering good competition), the Escort RS1600s were always 'best of the rest' – and there seemed to be so many of them. Although Ford gained no outright victories (Gardner, almost unbeatable, saw to that), one or other of the cars finished second overall in four races and third overall five times. As expected, Andy Rouse was the most successful individual driver. Once again, to quote *Autosport*: 'Rouse wiped up the 2-litre division of the British Touring Car Championship, almost toppling Frank Gardner from the overall title, and had a number of dices with Dave Brodie.'

Yet the season was marred at Silverstone in July, when Dave Brodie's RS1600 was involved in a huge accident, which also saw Dave Matthews's Broadspeed Capri RS2600 completely written off. Fortunately the drivers, though injured in the crash, both eventually recovered completely.

For 1973, Ford took the most advantage of the latest homologation provisions (which would run out at the end of the year), which allowed them to swap cylinder heads, by offering an ultra-small version of the BDA engine, and getting it approved for the 1.3-litre class. Vince Woodman and Gillian Fortescue-Thomas both drove what were effectively 'RS1300s' – though Ford never called them that, and of course you couldn't buy one from a Ford RS dealer – and Peter Hanson also had a privately-financed example!

These cars were invincible in their capacity class – and with 190bhp from 1.3-litres, this was to be expected (that was more power than the Broadspeed 1.6-litre Twin Cam had enjoyed as recently as 1970!) – and completely dominated throughout the year. Vince Woodman won five times and Peter Hanson four times. The highlight of an exciting season was that Hanson finished second overall at Ingliston, and fourth overall at Silverstone in the GP meeting.

And so it was that the Group 2 era came to an end at Brands Hatch in October 1973, coincidentally within days of the Energy Crisis erupting in the biggest possible way. It ended, as it had started, with Frank Gardner making all the running (and providing most of the tyre smoke when he spun off at South Bank corner) and, as so often in this hard-fought series, with a Ford Escort RS1600 (Andy Rouse driving) just 14 seconds away – in 20 laps – from outright victory.

For 1974, perhaps it really was time to return car specifications to something like normal – but if the RAC MSA thought this would reduce race speeds, they were much mistaken.

↑ When a new set of regulations – Group 2 – were imposed on the Championship for 1970, Frank Gardner imported a Ford 'Boss' Mustang from the USA, and turned it into a race winner.

← If only it had a larger and more powerful engine, in the early 1970s the Capri RS2600 could have been a regular winner in Group 2 BTCC races. Gerry Birrell (here seen at Brands Hatch in 1971) and Brian Muir drove the most consistently successful examples.

→ Frank Gardner's Chevrolet Camaro, sponsored by SCA Freight, was much the most successful 'tin-top' to race in the Group 2 category.

⬆ Although the SCA Freight Chevrolet Camaro was heavy, with a massive 5.7-litre/500bhp V8 engine, Frank Gardner's team made it handle very well indeed, and it won many races.

➡ One of the first successful Chevrolet Camaros was owned by Malcolm Gartlan, and driven by Brian Muir. Here he is on the way to winning the Tourist Trophy race in 1970.

◄ Frank Gardner was best described as a 'muscular driver', but sometimes his barging tactics didn't come off...

◄ In 1972 Brian Muir's 2.9-litre Ford Capri RS2600 was the equal of all but the most powerful American cars, and won several races. Muir also contested the Paul Ricard 6-hour race in France, and humbled the 'works' team!

⬇ In the early 1970s, BTCC regulations favoured outstanding 'class' cars, and Bill McGovern's Sunbeam Rallye Imp was certainly one of those. With preparation by George Bevan, this combination won the Championship in 1970, 1971 and 1972.

Impressive, right? 5.7 litres, 500bhp, Frank Gardner at the wheel of an immaculately prepared Chevrolet Camaro, meant that victory in 1973 was often assured.

Gerry Birrell was Ford's most versatile touring car racer in the early 1970s. Boreham built him this special 1.8-litre Escort RS1600 to race in selected BTCC events – this being Brands Hatch in 1972.

For 1970 Broadspeed built this 145bhp Ford Escort 1300GT for John Fitzpatrick to race in the BTCC, when he won his class and finished third overall.

↑ In 1971 Broadspeed built this state-of-the-art Escort RS1600 for John Fitzpatrick to drive in the BTCC. It had an eventful season, including two big crashes – but outright wins too.

↖ In 1970 EVX 248H, a Broadspeed Ford Escort Twin-Cam, was usually Chris Craft's car for the BTCC series, but Jackie Stewart drove it in the first leg of the two-part Tourist Trophy race too.

← Time to work, time to play – during the week Rod Mansfield worked at Ford's AVO factory, developing special Escort RS models, but at weekends he raced this Escort Twin-Cam in the BTCC, with some distinction.

⬆ In 1971 Vince Woodman drove this highly successful Ford Escort GT, a car which came from Broadspeed, with all the expertise that the Warwickshire car builder could muster.

↗ If Bill McGovern's Sunbeam Rallye Imp had not been so metronomically reliable, Dave Matthews' Escort RS1600 would surely have won the Championship in 1972; as it was he had to settle for a class win, and second overall.

➡ Broadspeed Capri versus Gardner/SCA Freight Chevrolet Camaro in 1973 – where the Camaro usually won because of its colossal power. The Capri was written off in a huge accident at Silverstone, but happily the driver (Dave Matthews) recovered.

⬆Brands Hatch in 1972, where Vince Woodman had this smart Broadspeed/Esso supported Escort RS1600.

➡The sign-writing on the flanks tells it all, for in 1973 Ford somehow homologated a 1.3-litre BDA-engined version of the Escort, producing a high-revving, 190bhp projectile, which quite dominated the BTCC class. Vince Woodman, Peter Hanson and Gillian Fortescue-Thomas all enjoyed these cars while they could, for a change of regulations outlawed them for 1974.

Starting in 1974, cars in the Saloon Car Championship would run in the FIA Group 1 category – or at least the RAC MSA's version of that category – which, according to the hopes of the somewhat naïve administrators, would bring them much closer to 'showroom specification' then ever before.

Entrants and factories committed to support saloon car racing, though, had other ideas. Year after year, more and more features would be homologated to particular cars (some of them, frankly, on very sketchy grounds, with little proved as to numbers built), which gradually gave them more and more performance. In addition to that, and in response to pressure from manufacturers and entrants, the RAC MSA relaxed its own regulations (it eventually allowed alternative carburation, for instance, though changes to the cylinder head castings were forbidden), imposing something nicknamed Group '1½' in the final years.

The result (and has it ever been otherwise?) was that vehicle performance moved ahead rapidly in later seasons. Typical, in many ways, was that in 1974 Ford Motorsport's own Capri II 3-litre (for Tom Walkinshaw to drive) was catalogued with 138bhp and produced 175bhp on the race track, while things progressed so far that in 1980 the identically-engined Capri III 3-litres had 255bhp.

It was the same story with the 16-valve 2-litre Triumph Dolomite Sprints from Broadspeed, on which Ralph Broad and Andy Rouse worked their magic. Catalogued with 127bhp, the 1974 cars raced with 174bhp, but by 1978 Tony Dron's car ran with 215bhp and was often capable of beating the Capris for outright victories.

In one major respect, though, the change to Group 1 brought new cars, and some new faces, into the sport. Des O'Dell of Chrysler UK, as adept at reading – and reacting – to regulations as anyone else in the business, developed 1.3-litre Chrysler Avenger GTs so well that Bernard Unett won the Championship three times, Richard Longman then found ways of going even faster in a 1.3-litre Mini 1275GT, and Win Percy also won the series twice using rotary-engined Mazda RX7s (saloons – give us a break, that had to be a leg-pull!) prepared by Tom Walkinshaw Racing.

All this, of course, was achieved because of the perverse points scoring system, which favoured cars that were outstanding in their class, rather than those that won races outright. How can we prove this? By showing that 3-litre-engined Ford Capris won no fewer than 57 races in nine years – Gordon Spice being the most successful individual driver – yet a Capri driver never came close to becoming Champion.

In 1974, though, there was much variety to be written about, although one of five different Chevrolet Camaros still dominated the overall results, with Stuart Graham's 5.7-litre Z28 the most successful. Walkinshaw's Capri was often battling against Opel Commodores or BMW CSis, while Andy Rouse's Broadspeed Triumph Dolomite Sprint went head to head with Barrie Williams's rotary-engined Mazda RX3, which beat it several times. Gerry Marshall and Tim Stock raced Vauxhall Magnum Coupés, which were not quick enough. Bernard Unett's immaculately-prepared Chrysler/Hillman Avenger GT was dominant in the 1.6-litre class, but John Markey also figured in a Toyota Celica GT.

What was interesting was that by reverting to Group 1 (or 'Gp 1½' as some journalists insisted on calling it, right from the start), the RAC MSA outlawed every competitive Ford Escort, for Ford was not interested in Gp 1, as the rather rare 16-valve cars could not be homologated in that category.

Things became fiercely more competitive in 1975, when Stuart Graham fitted a 7.4-litre V8 engine to his Camaro (and Vince Woodman followed suit later in the year), while Broadspeed produced a 16-valve Triumph engine which could develop 235bhp in events outside the Championship, and a very consistent 185–190bhp when running to British supervised rules. Andy Rouse and journalist Roger Bell drove the cars, but because Rouse was consistently a class winner, he piled up the points to win the Championship, though it was the usual thundering phalanx of Camaros that took individual race victories.

At the end of the year, presumably when he had run out of new things to say about the same faces, commentating guru Ian Titchmarsh noted that the so-called sponsor (Sydney Miller) had promised lots of dosh from his company, Southern Organs, but had then disappeared from the face of the earth before the end of the season, and had apparently never paid over his promised sponsorship dues.

Titchmarsh, in any case, seemed to be suffering from saloon car fatigue, calling the series, '...that great institution which has gradually meant less and less as the years have passed since the RAC took it away from the BRSCC... This championship carried an insignificance never previously attained. Events were run at anything from the British GP to Ingliston clubbies, and foreign participation was precisely nil because no-one else built cars to the same regulations.'

Ian must have been having a grumpy day when he wrote those provocative words, for a year later, when surveying the same cars which had raced in 1976, he would comment that: '...there is no doubt that saloon cars attract much of the casual spectator's attention, and play a very important part in any promoter's programme. The trouble is that, with so many different types of car involved, it is very difficult to equate performance... Nowhere were the problems better demonstrated than in the RAC British Touring Car Championship, for which Auntie found sponsorship from Keith Prowse at the last minute...'

Through no fault of their own, one could never expect 200bhp of Capri to beat 550bhp of Chevrolet unless there was no grip in monsoon weather conditions (not often found in 1975). Ford had not won a single race in 1975. This, however, all changed in 1976, for all the big-engined American cars had been outlawed by a change in regulations, which left the Capris (led more often than not by Gordon Spice) fighting it out with Ralph Broad's Dolomite Sprints.

Even so, these were more effective Capris than ever, for inventive homologation had provided them with a different camshaft profile, a closer-ratio gearbox with Hewland internals, and bigger brakes. Not only that, but Ford somehow got a 'Higher Performance Engine (High Altitude Territories)' approved, where the nominal compression ratio was 10.25:1. Did anyone ever see one of these 'standard' cars in a showroom? Doubtful – and certainly not in 'high altitude' territories like Bolivia or Nepal...

The result was that in 1976 the Capris won all ten of the Championship races – four each to Gordon Spice and Tom Walkinshaw, one each for Vince Woodman and Colin Vandervell – but that sort of close competition meant that it would be another, class-dominant, car – Bernard Unett's 1.3-litre Chrysler Avenger GT – which took the Championship trophy once again.

Although most of the same cars, and indeed most of the same names, reappeared in 1977, the character somehow began to get back into this Championship. For sure, every event in the 12-car series might have been contested by one of a handful of 3-litre engined Capris, but these were significantly faster than before.

Another tide of inventive homologation – by Ford and by Broadspeed/Triumph saw the flavour enriched in 1977. It was only the RAC MSA's rather special and relaxed attitude to its own Group '1½' regulations that allowed the Dolomite Sprints to use twin dual-choke Weber carburettors (205bhp from a normally-aspirated 2-litre engine in so-called Group 1½-trim), a close-ratio gearbox and bigger ventilated disc brakes, while the Capris could use a new front spoiler, a quick rack, and an anti-dive front suspension geometry kit.

The result was that competition was very fierce indeed, with Tony Dron's Dolomite winning several races outright. The Capris, even though fresher than before, only won six times, but because this was with five different drivers (there was no question of favouritism, or a single 'works' sponsored car in their ranks), none of them looked like challenging for the Championship crown.

Because there was such vigorous competition in all the classes, the destination of the 1977 Trophy was in doubt up to the very last round at Brands Hatch. The Dolomite faced strong competition from Gerry Marshall and Jeff Allam (Vauxhall Magnums), Richard Lloyd's VW Golf GTi had to fight it out with Brian Pepper's VW and Martin Brundle's Toyota Celica GT, while Bernard Unett (1.3-litre Chrysler Avenger) was finally faced with real competition from Richard Longman in a Mini 1275GT (he could not use a Mini-Cooper S, as that car had been out of production for six years).

If Longman had had the use of a Mini-Cooper S, things might have been different, but even so, his battles with Bernard Unett's 'works' Avenger GT1300 were stirring. As commentator/journalist Robin Bradford later commented, 'Time and again the green-and-white Avenger and the blue Mini would come out of a corner with less than a coat of paint separating them, and these two provided some of the most exciting racing of the season, away from the top class struggles.'

This should not, of course, demean the performance of the Unett/Avenger/Chrysler-UK programme, in what was theoretically a too-heavy, under-powered machine. Unett had cut his teeth in Rallye Imps, then in an ex-works Sunbeam Tiger, before turning to the Avenger. Because he was not only race-experienced, but ultra-smooth, and also worked as a development engineer in the Chrysler Competitions Department, Unett was the right man for the job. This was his third outright Championship victory (though Tony Dron ran him desperately close), but also his last, as Chrysler then turned back to International rallying, and the funds dried up.

The iniquities of the Championship's point-scoring system were never so apparent as in 1978, when Capris won ten races, Gordon Spice won six of those races, yet he could do no better than finish fourth in the points standings. Although the fleet of Capris were upgraded from

Capri II to Capri III (four headlamps, slight front-end style changes, and a transverse spoiler, which was a marginal improvement – almost all of them using conversion kits supplied by Ford to update existing Capri IIs!), they still only had 220bhp, and the performance of the chassis was much the same as ever.

Tom Walkinshaw's BMW 530i was valiant, but far too heavy (which wasn't Tom's fault), and as far as the spectators were concerned it was otherwise the same as before, with Tony Dron's Broadspeed Dolomite, Richard Lloyd's VW Golf GTi and Richard Longman's Mini 1275GT all running away with their classes.

Even though the Capris still held a stranglehold on British saloon car racing, real novelties were on the horizon at the end of the decade. Noisiest and most extrovert by far was Tom Walkinshaw's rotary-engined Mazda RX7, which made mince-meat of its conventional (Triumph Dolomite Sprint) rivals in the 2.3-litre class. Controversial because of its dimensions (was it really a four-seater?), its rotary engine (which some said should have been rated at higher than 2.3-litres), and its non-saloon reputation, it was a real talking point throughout the year – come to think of it, anything with which Walkinshaw was linked usually was.

Although Capris won 11 of the 12 races (the Mazda RX7 won the other), it was Richard Longman's Mini 1275GT, which won its class ten times, that easily won the Championship.

This was all too much for the RAC MSA, who then re-shuffled their rules again for 1980. Not only did they apply higher minimum weight limits (which killed off the Minis), but cars of up to 3,500cc were allowed to take part. To this day, no-one knows how it was achieved, but V8-powered Rover SD1s, normally catalogued at 3,528cc, were homologated at 3,492cc ('minimum-tolerance bore and stroke, old boy'), and soon started winning. Although the ageing Capri won nine races, the Rover won once, and looked threatening. Although Win Percy's Mazda RX7 won every single 2.3-litre class, it was quite overshadowed by the Capri–Rover battle.

In 1981, therefore, for the Capris it was almost Game Over, for they were no faster than before, whereas the Rovers won all of the last six races. Peter Lovett and Jeff Allam shared the Rover glory, though as usual with this Championship's points scoring system it was the ever-consistent Win Percy (Mazda RX7) who habitually won the 2.3-litre class, and won the Championship.

Then came 1982, the last of the 'Group 1' series (for the RAC MSA soon let it be known that they would be adopting Group A regulations in 1983), where Rover continued to dominate, and only Vince Woodman's old Capri III could make much impression on them. By winning his class in every single one of the 12 races, Win Percy secured his third consecutive Championship and – guess who – Richard Longman changed his car yet again (this time it was a Metro) to win the 1.3-litre class.

And so, on 3 October 1982, the last Group 1 race of all was held, nine seasons after it had been set up in the UK. In all that time, there were new faces – notably Richard Longman, Win Percy and Andy Rouse – controversy over the eligibility of cars like the Mazda RX7 and the Rover 3500, but one car had been, and remained, a race-winner throughout: the 3-litre Capri. Even so, it was to fall spectacularly from grace in 1983.

⬆ Early in his BTCC career, Andy Rouse drove Ralph Broad's Triumph Dolomite Sprints to many a race victory in the mid-1970s. He won the Championship outright in 1975.

↗ Chrysler had already developed the Avenger GT for saloon car racing in 1973 (the Group 1 cars appearing in the Castrol Group 1 series), before near identical cars were prepared for Bernard Unett (here seen at the wheel) to drive in the RAC Castrol-sponsored BTCC of 1974.

➡ Respected journalist Roger Bell (of *Motor*) was the second driver in the Broadspeed Triumph Dolomite team of 1975.

↑ Ralph Broad (left) was not only a brilliant engineer, but a forceful team manager too – here seen giving instructions to driver Roger Bell before one of the 1975 races in the BTCC.

↘ Brands Hatch in 1975, with Roger Bell's Broadspeed Triumph Dolomite Sprint ahead of one of the rotary-engined Mazda RX3s.

← Awful track conditions at Mallory Park in 1975, with Andy Rouse (Broadspeed Triumph Dolomite Sprint) ahead of team-mate Roger Bell. Rouse won the BTCC Championship in that year.

↑ Vauxhall came into the sport in the 1970s, with 2.3-litre engined Magnum Coupés, driven by heroes like Gerry Marshall, but they never had the power to match that of the all-conquering Capris of the period.

↖ Tom Walkinshaw's Capri II won four BTCC races in 1976, his car being sponsored by Hermetite and Castrol. Along with Gordon Spice, Walkinshaw was one of the most successful Capri drivers of this period.

↙ Gordon Spice, here seen leading the Capri pack in the support race at the British F1 GP meeting at Silverstone in the mid-1970s, was the most successful Capri driver of all.

⬆ Ford first dabbled with Group '1½' by preparing this Capri for Tom Walkinshaw to drive in 1974: he won two races.

⬉ When it came to getting publicity, Ford's PR people rarely missed a trick. In 1978, when the Capri III had just started its racing career, they posed the Gordon Spice car alongside an X-pack equipped Capri road car.

⬅ When the BTCC was running according to Group '1½' regulations, Ford's 3-litre car was a regular winner, with cars driven by Gordon Spice being the most successful of all. This was Gordon, in his newly-homologated Capri III, at Oulton Park in 1979.

⬆ Chris Craft was a formidable Capri racer, not only in 3000GT Mk IIs, but in the Mk IIIs that followed. Sponsorship on this car was by Hammonds Chop Sauce – a food products company from Yorkshire, whose boss was a rabid motorsport fanatic.

↗ Gordon Spice won more British races in one of his Capri 3000GTs than any other driver of the period. This was Silverstone in the mid-1970s...

→ ...and here again is the self-same car, but with a subtly different livery and sponsorship job.

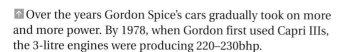 Over the years Gordon Spice's cars gradually took on more and more power. By 1978, when Gordon first used Capri IIIs, the 3-litre engines were producing 220–230bhp.

→ New regulations, new name, new car – and new success in 1974, when the RAC MSA adopted Group '1½'. Driving a 'works' Chrysler Avenger 1600GT, Bernard Unett was outstanding in his class, and won the series.

PAGES 106–107 A typical start line traffic jam in 1976, with Tom Walkinshaw's and Gordon Spice's Capri 3000GTs bracketing Tony Dron's Triumph Dolomite Sprint on the front row, one lonely-looking Vauxhall Magnum Coupé and several other Capris close behind.

In 1976 and 1977 Bernard Unett's Chrysler Avenger 1300 GT wasn't the fastest car of all, but was outstanding in its class.

In the mid-1970s, British Leyland commissioned Broadspeed to turn the new Triumph Dolomite Sprint into a race winner. This was Tony Dron's car on the start line at Silverstone in 1975, with new motorsport supremo John Davenport holding the car's door.

Driving this Broadspeed Triumph Dolomite Sprint, Andy Rouse won the 1975 Championship by the narrowest of margins, then went on to drive the huge 'works' Jaguars in Europe.

⬆ With more help from the VW factory, Richard Lloyd's Golf GTI might have been even more successful, though it was still a very competitive 1.6-litre machine.

⬈ Behind the Capris, the Mini 1275GT, Dolomite Sprint, Toyota Celica and VW Scirocco models all show off the variety of Group '1½' racing in the late 1970s.

➔ Richard Longman used the 'class advantage' regulations to his advantage in 1978 and 1979, when his 1.3-litre engine Mini 1275GT became overall Champion.

⬆ Tom Walkinshaw was close to Mazda in the late 1970s, winning his class and finishing second in the Championship in this rotary-engined RX7 in 1979.

◥ Colour schemes come and go, but Win Percy's rotary-engined Mazda RX7 kept going hard, to win the Championship outright in 1980 and 1981. But how on earth was this car ever homologated as a four-seater?

⬅ The old order changed eventually and by the early 1980s the Capri 3000GT (second in line) had been matched by the rotary-engined TWR Mazdas, and the Rover SD1 (third in the queue) was shaping up to pass both of them.

1983–1990

GROUP A, WITH REAL POWER

As far as the BTCC was concerned, from 1983 it was all-change. Like the rest of world motorsport, the RAC MSA dropped obsolete regulations (Group 1 in this case) and imposed new ones (Group A) in their place. At the time they could have had no idea of the power race they were about to unleash.

Broadly speaking, similar-engined first-generation Group A cars were as fast as the best Group 2 cars had become by the 1980s, though car makers had to build 5,000 cars (not 1,000 as in the old Group 2) to gain homologation. Although Group A allowed more technical freedoms in the chassis, there was no allowance for alternative carburation.

There was, however, a major innovation. Under Group A, car makers could then produce a 500-off evolution. Car-makers like BMW and Mercedes-Benz would all embrace this concession, but it was Ford who really trumped every other ace with their turbocharged Sierras.

For comparison and in summary, in 1982 the best of the 3-litre Capris produced 255bhp, the first of the turbocharged Sierra RS Cosworths produced 340bhp in 1986, but the 'evolution' Sierra RS500 Cosworth of 1987–1990 produced up to 550bhp (from a 2-litre engine). Once the RS500 Cosworths had become reliable, it was all over as far as any other marque and model was concerned.

All this, though, would come to pass in the second half of the 1980s, for in the first two years every entrant looked around for the best first-generation Group A cars that could be found. Ford, for a short time, was out of contention, and originally the most competitive machines were the latest big Rovers – Vitesses with fuel injection and 190bhp in showroom form – and the Alfa Romeo GTV6 with a highly-tuneable 2.5-litre engine and 160bhp as standard.

Thereafter, the BTCC reverted to 'Formula Ford' once again. Andy Rouse's Merkur (Sierra) XR4Ti dominated the scene in 1985 and 1986, the Sierra RS500 Cosworth took over in 1987 (Rouse mainly, then Rob Gravett), and not even the technical might of BMW could make the normally-aspirated 2.3-litre M3s competitive. In 1990 the RS500 was still so far ahead of any of its rivals that the RAC MSA felt that it had to change the entire format for the 1990s.

The story of the first, 1983, season is quickly told, though its technical manoeuvrings could take up an entire chapter. Tom Walkinshaw's TWR organisation built three 'works' Rovers, which had more than 300bhp. These then won every one of the eleven qualifying races (Steve Soper won five times, Peter Lovett four times and Jeff Allam twice), their major competition coming from Andy Rouse, who took over Pete Hall's newly-prepared Alfa Romeo GTV6.

Unhappily, a great deal of personal animosity between Walkinshaw and Frank Sytner (who ran a BMW 635CSi), ruined everything, for Sytner seemed determined to find homologation irregularities in the Rovers, and vice versa. This was to no-one's advantage, the dispute went on for months, all the way up to an official inquiry led by Lord (once Sir Hartley) Shawcross, and it was not until June 1984 (eight months after the end of the Championship) that Rover, and TWR, washed its hands of the whole business, 'disassociated' its team from the Championship, and allowed Rouse's class-winning Alfa Romeo to win by default.

In the meantime, Ford came back strongly with Escort RS1600is in the 1.6-litre class, Austin-Rover's turbocharged MG Metros (rated as 1.8-litre cars by the 'turbo performance factor') proved to be immensely entertaining, and oddities like a Colt Starion Turbo (Dave Brodie) and a Toyota Celica Supra (Win Percy) added spice.

The after-shocks of this lengthy dispute ran on so long that it skewed the 1984 Championship as well. For 1984 Andy Rouse built up a new Rover Vitesse, proceeded to match and sometimes beat the 'works' Rovers early in the year, before the 'works' cars were abruptly withdrawn after six races, of which they had won twice. Rouse eventually won six times and finished second four times, with amazing consistency, while Frank Sytner continued to campaign his BMW 635 CSi, but never won at all.

To everyone's amazement, Dave Brodie's turbocharged Colt won one race – the last round at Silverstone – and cars like Graham Goode's Nissan Bluebird Turbo (four 2.5-litre class wins), and Richard Longman's Datapost-sponsored Ford Escort RS1600i (six class wins) brought a great deal of interest to the mid-field. Tony Pond's 'works' MG Metro Turbo (still rated as a 1.8-litre) won three classes before being abruptly withdrawn by Austin-Rover, which rather killed off competition in the 2.5-litre category.

After the dramas of 1983 and 1984, the BTCC suffered something of a slump in the next two seasons. Not a slump in performance, you understand (Andy Rouse in a 340bhp Ford/Merkur XR4Ti saw to that), but in competition, where there were no longer any truly competitive Rovers. Dave Brodie's Colt Starion Turbo was one of the surprises of the year – he won once and was always competitive – and, once he got it homologated and sorted out, Richard Longman's Ford Escort RS Turbo (240bhp from just 1.6-litres) provided some real fireworks.

Austin-Rover didn't figure in 1985 because it was putting most of its effort behind the Metro 6R4 in rallying, while TWR was totally engrossed with Jaguar XJSs in the European series. This meant that Andy Rouse (who had been attracted to a Merkur XR4Ti programme by Ford, with promises of the Sierra RS Cosworth to follow in 1987) had little outright competition.

The ICS-sponsored Merkur – a Sierra XR4i-lookalike, really, but with an American turbocharged 2.3-litre engine – was the right car for the right time, for with the same all-independent suspension that the RS Cosworth was also going to use this made it an ideal test bed – though Andy always admitted that it was an interim model. No matter, in 1985 he won nine of the 12 races outright – and won the Championship for the third successive year, each of those wins being in a different make and model of car.

Turbocharging, as seen in Rouse's Merkur/Ford, in Brodie's Colt and in Longman's Escort, was clearly going to be even more important in future years. However, as far as the rest of a car's chassis was concerned, equally large advances would be needed. As Joe Saward wrote in his end-of-term report in November 1985: 'Richard Longman campaigned the Ford Escort RS Turbo when it eventually received its homologation, which was not until June. Thereafter he scored three class wins with the car, which exhibited truly breathtaking straight-line speed, if a dislike of slowing down or turning corners. When the car is fully developed, it is going to be very hard to beat...'

In almost every way, though, the 1986 season was the lull before the storm (both the Sierra RS Cosworth and the BMW M3 were due to arrive in 1987), and interest and publicity slumped to a low. Although Rouse's standards were as high as ever – need one say that the Ford/Merkur dominated the series, with five outright race victories? – there were really only a dozen stalwarts who turned up for round after round. Only 14 cars started the season's first race, and only 11 started at Donington in mid-year.

It wasn't long before Rouse's Ford/Merkur, Chris Hodgetts' Toyota Corolla and Richard Longman's Escort RS Turbo took over at the top of the points table, and stayed there throughout the year.

Then, in 1987, came the new dawn, where Dunlop picked up overall sponsorship, and contributed a great deal of promotion. Ford got the Sierra RS Cosworth homologated at the start of the season, as did BMW the M3, and the monstrously powerful Sierra RS500 Cosworth followed in August, to contest the last five races. There was never any question of cheating with the RS500s – for every single car in that 500-off batch was built (by Aston Martin Tickford, at Bedworth, near Coventry), and every one was signed off by the inspectors before 'Evolution' homologation was secured.

Amazingly, the Sierra Cosworth took a few months to find its feet – reliability of the turbocharged engines, and the hard-worked transmissions was an issue at first – but once the cars started winning, the results of each and every BTCC race until the end of 1990 was entirely predictable. And it was not just one driver and one car either – by the end of the decade Andy Rouse, Robb Gravett, Steve Soper, Graham Goode, Laurence Bristow and Tim Harvey were all in potential race winning cars, all with 500bhp and more under the bonnet, and on many occasions there were ten or even more Sierras at the front of the grid after qualifying.

TV coverage had arrived by this time, and a great deal of careful editing was often needed to make the races look less processional than they actually were. If there had not been a great deal of mano-a-mano scrapping for position (who will ever forget the Rouse versus Soper or Rouse versus Gravett battles of this period?) it might have been very difficult to spice up the coverage.

From 1987 to 1990, therefore, it was never a question of which make of car would win individual races – it would invariably be a Sierra RS500 Cosworth – but from year to year the main interest was in discovering which would be a dominant car in the smaller engine-capacity classes, and would therefore be expected to win the Championship itself. Because there was so much close fighting in the 'Sierra class' (Andy Rouse had a hand in preparing several concurrent machines in his own and his rivals' teams!), all of which were closely competitive, until 1990 there would be no dominant car/driver in that category.

Race results in 1987, frankly, were skewed because four-times Champion Andy Rouse did not contest every event. With his sights on the World Touring Car Championship (an infamous series in which the Swiss-based Eggenberger RS500 Cosworths totally obliterated its opposition towards the end of the year), Andy missed half the rounds – but still notched up three outright wins.

This was the final year in which a Rover Vitesse (complete with twin-plenum injection system atop the 'under 3.5-litre' engine) was competitive, and it clocked up four victories. Sierras won six times, Mike O'Brien's 5.0-litre Holden Commodore once, and James Weaver's BMW 635CSi once. Even so it was Chris 'the Mad Monk' Hodgetts and his Toyota Corolla GT which recorded class wins in ten of the 12 races to win the Championship on points. Frank Sytner won three classes in his BMW M3 in the second half of the season, which, if we had only known it, was a real portent for 1988.

There were two main battles in 1988 – Andy Rouse versus other Sierras for outright victories, and Frank Sytner versus Mike Smith (both in Prodrive BMW M3s) in the 2.5-litre class. It was no surprise to see Sytner lifting the trophy, by winning his class on all but one occasion.

Mike Smith, the victim of team orders, and less than pleased at this, later stormed off to found a Sierra team for 1989, while not even Mr Consistency Rouse himself (nine race victories) could match that, though Andy comprehensively beat the Eggenberger car, which produced just two wins – one for Steve Soper, one for Gianfranco Brancatelli.

Although the Sierras continued to win all the races in 1989, there was real needle between Rouse's team and that of Trakstar (Rob Gravett and Mike Smith) where tyres – Pirelli (Rouse) and Yokohama (Trakstar) – were important features. Frank Sytner and James Weaver (BMW M3s) were equally as spectacular, but totally outgunned – 350 bhp could never battle with 550bhp. Because of the points scoring system employed, then, it was no surprise that John Cleland's 16-valve Vauxhall Astra won his class and the overall title.

For the RAC MSA, and for Esso, as sponsors, the message in 1989 was that real competition, at several levels, was always going to be present, so spectator numbers and TV viewing figures continued to grow.

Behind the scenes, though, there was disquiet. Unless someone imported a competitive Group A Nissan Skyline (which was a winning car on the Pacific Rim) there was no sign of the Sierras ever being beaten. For 1990, therefore, the MSA opened up a second front, for 2-litre cars, which would run to different regulations.

And so it was. In 1990, the pace of the Sierras was at its peak, while the 2-litre class, though less rapid, was close-fought between BMW's re-engined M3s and Vauxhall's newly-developed Cavaliers. As to the Sierras, though Trakstar almost went broke before the season started, when their sponsor reneged on an agreement, they concentrated all efforts on Robb Gravett's car. Helped along by Yokohama tyres, and a Mountune engine, Robb won nine races against four from Andy Rouse – and became the first 'big-engined' driver to win the Championship outright since 1985.

The 2-litre cars (with no more than 280–290bhp) always fought hard among themselves, the final result being five class victories for Sytner's BMW M3 against four for John Cleland's Vauxhall Cavalier.

At the end of the year, therefore, the RAC MSA abandoned its Group A category, and would concentrate on Super Touring Cars in future. There was no future for Sierras – having won the 1987 World series, that was canned, and having won the European series in 1988, that was canned too. Now every national series was being closed to the all-conquering Fords too. Excellence was being banned – was that justice?

⬆ Even before Ford produced the Sierra RS500 Cosworth, an earlier model, the Ford (Merkur) XR4Ti dominated the BTCC. Cars built by Andy Rouse won the majority of races in 1985 and 1986. Here the two team cars – driven by Andy Rouse and David Sears – finish nose to tail to win a race at Brands Hatch in 1986.

◤ Vauxhall read the BTCC regulations very carefully in the late 1980s and concluded that a well-prepared 'class' car could win the Championship. They were right – in 1989 this Astra GT/E, driven by John Cleland was a consistent class winner, ably backed up by Louise Aitken-Walker. The RS500s might have been winning all the races, but it was Cleland who notched up all the points.

◄ Frank Sytner's Mobil BMW falls foul of Snetterton's Russell Chicane in 1990, the first year of the 2-litre class and the year before it became the basis of the entire championship.

In 1988 Andy Rouse's Sierra RS500 Cosworths were the fastest in the Championship. Andy won nine races, and finished third in the series.

Andy Rouse worked his Sierra RS500s extremely hard during the 1987 season. Apart from competing in the BTCC, he also found time to enter it in the Tourist Trophy race (at Silverstone), where it ran in this unique colour scheme.

By the end of the 1980s the fastest of all the Sierra RS500 Cosworths was this Trakstar example, driven by Robb Gravett, which won the series in 1990 after a season-long battle with Andy Rouse's Sierra.

⬆ Having won the 1983 Championship in an Alfa Romeo GTV6, Andy Rouse then prepared a Rover Vitesse for 1984, which was equally as effective as the works-backed TWR cars which later withdrew from the series. Andy won the Championship in this car.

↗ In 1985 and 1986 Andy Rouse's Ford Merkur Sierra XR4Ti was the fastest of all the BTCC cars of this period, for it ran with a 320bhp turbocharged 2.3-litre engine.

➡ By the mid-1980s the Capris were obsolete, but this car is trying its best to stay with Andy Rouse's XR4Ti as it rounds Lodge Corner at Oulton Park in 1985.

⬆ By 1984, Richard Longman's Datapost-sponsored Escort RS1600is were often seen nose to tail on BTCC circuits. If Richard's car stayed so close to the car in front for much longer, the radiator must surely have overheated!

⬉ Although the Toyota Celica Supra was beautifully-prepared, and well-driven by Win Percy in 1984, it could not keep up with the more powerful cars in the BTCC series.

⬅ By 1984 Tony Pond's Group A MG Metro Turbo was class-competitive – reputedly it had at least 180bhp driving through the front wheels – but when Austin-Rover withdrew from the series all its chances were lost.

⬆ Group A didn't mean showroom-standard – not by a long way, this Datapost Escort being a typical BTCC interior of the mid-1980s.

⬉ Turbocharging made a mockery of potential Touring Car racing outputs in the 1980s. In 1985 and 1986 Richard Longman drove a Ford Escort RS Turbo which, even with only a 1.6-litre engine and rated at 132bhp in the showroom, could race with up to 270bhp! Stopping it, though, could be a problem...

⬅ BTCC contenders like the Datapost Escort RS Turbo found time to compete in the RAC Tourist Trophy race as well. In 1986 Richard Longman's car gave a hard time to one of the turbocharged Volvos.

↑ In the BTCC it helps to have a good test driver! Triple F1 World Champion Jackie Stewart found time to test Longman's Escort RS Turbo in 1986.

↗ Jeff Allam and Steve Soper dominated many BTCC races in 1983 in their TWR-prepared Rover Vitesses, only to be thrown out after a prolonged series of eligibility protests. If they had survived these traumas, Soper would have been BTCC champion, and Allam third.

⇒ What a pity that scrutineering arguments got in the way of motor racing in the early 1980s. As run by TWR, this was one of the extremely smart 3.5-litre Rover Vitesses that won so many races in 1983 and 1984, before Austin-Rover suddenly withdrew from the series.

TWR built the fastest and most stable Rover Vitesses of all in the early 1980s, with Steve Soper one of their most outstanding drivers.

⬆ In 1989 John Cleland and Louise Aitken-Walker drove Vauxhall Astra GT/Es to many class victories in the BTCC – this car being just ahead of a VW Golf GTi.

⬉ In the last event of 1983, at Silverstone, Steve Soper led home Jeff Allam to a 1–2 finish in their Rover Vitesses.

⬅ Steve Soper was the fastest of several super-committed drivers in TWR-built Rover Vitesses in 1983 and 1984.

When the BTCC embraced Group A regulations for 1983 Andy Rouse read the regulations very carefully, concluded that a V6-engined Alfa Romeo GTV6 might be supreme – and proved. Although he had to battle with the TWR Rover Vitesses throughout the year, he was eventually crowned Champion.

Thruxton in 1989, with John Cleland's 1.8-litre Vauxhall Astra GT/E setting to fight for another 2-litre class win.

John Cleland (Vauxhall Astra GT/E) just ahead of Phil Dowsett's Toyota Corolla GT, in 1989.

⬆ Throughout 1983, the TWR Rovers fought a running battle among themselves, and with the scrutineers. Though they won most of the races during the season, they were eventually thrown out of the series on homologation grounds, and withdrew from the Championship.

⬅ In 1990 the RAC set up a separate 2-litre class, as a prelude to the Special Touring Cars category that was to follow. BMW and Vauxhall took it all very seriously, with Frank Sytner's BMW M3 winning that category.

PAGES 136–137 Between 1988 and 1990, you needed a 500bhp-plus Sierra RS500 Cosworth to be competitive in the BTCC. On the grid, and ready to start the Thruxton race, Steve Soper (Texaco-Eggenberger) and Andy Rouse (Kaliber), are ahead of at least ten more Sierras, for the BMW M3s could not cope with this much sheer power.

⬆ For a short period, BTCC cars raced on a street circuit in Birmingham. This is Steve Soper, in one of the spectacularly-styled Eggenberger Sierra RS500 Cosworths, which fought so many times with Andy Rouse's 'Kaliber' car in 1988.

◤ Real power on the grid at Thruxton in 1988, where Andy Rouse's 500bhp Ford Sierra RS500 Cosworth prepares to do battle with a fleet of 'fast Fords'.

⬅ Trakstar began racing Sierra RS500 Cosworths in 1989, but it was in 1990 that this car, raced so brilliantly by Robb Gravett, won most races and won the Championship.

1991–2000

SUPER TOURING CARS

Except for the Group 5 era of the late 1960s, no British Touring Car race period was as exciting, or as close-fought, as that of the 1990s, when the BTCC ran to the 'Super Touring Cars' formula. This was a period in which all eligible cars had to run with normally-aspirated 2-litre engines (which would be rev-limited to 8,500rpm).

Free in some respects, but heavily restricted in others, the regulations produced very close racing, but at very high prices to entrants. The formula which attracted up to ten manufacturers at one stage gradually throttled itself because of high cost.

Authorised by the RAC MSA, to appease other manufacturers whose cars could not match the Ford Sierra RS500 Cosworths in the 1980s, the Super Touring Car formula set out to make all things possible for those willing to spend the money. As spelt out in the summer of 1989, for the 1990 BTCC, this new 2-litre category demanded:

■ Four-seater saloons, at least 13ft 9in./4.2m long.
■ Cars to be versions of those where more than 5,000 had been built in the previous 12 months.
■ Engines to be 2-litre, normally aspirated units. Existing power units could be enlarged, or reduced in capacity, to suit this limit.
■ Engines to be from that manufacturer's range (if necessary, from the parent company's products, anywhere in the world, not just in the country where racing took place – which was good news for GM or Ford), but not necessarily from the chosen model range.
■ Two-wheel drive to be the norm, though front-drive cars could run 221lb/100kg lighter than rear-drive cars.
■ Tyre treads were limited to not more than 9in/229mm wide.
■ To equate different traction performance, the minimum weight for front-wheel drive cars was to be 950kg, that of rear-drive cars 1,050kg.

BMW and Vauxhall were attracted and other manufacturers sat on the fence at first. Even so, for 1991 the RAC MSA decided to impose it as the new template for British saloon car racing. An independent new company, TOCA (TOuring Car Association), ran the entire series and the regulations were tweaked a little, to encourage manufacturers with four-wheel-drive machines to compete.

The first specially-developed Super Tourers would not appear until 1993, and at first it was Vauxhall and BMW which made all the running. Having had their all-conquering Sierras shot from under them, Ford made it clear that they were not in a hurry to return, so their previous runners had to scramble to find alternative cars to drive for two or three years, while other manufacturers – Renault in particular – were slow to build proper racing cars, in the game of musical chairs which followed.

None had forecast that the ever-resourceful Andy Rouse could turn the previously unknown Toyota Carina into a very competent, race-winning car. Accordingly, at the end of a season in which no fewer than 16 M3 pilots scored points, Vauxhall's John Cleland won three races, as did Andy Rouse's Toyota. Championship winner Will Hoy – his M3 being run by the Vic Lee team, with the Listerine support that used to grace a Sierra RS500 – won three races, but stood on the podium a further six times.

Because of the engine tuning limitations, every competitive car had about 300bhp, and as their handling was demonstrably better than that of the late-1980s Sierras, they were very fast around the circuits too. By the mid-1990s, the Super Touring Cars would be faster than the 550bhp RS500s had ever been.

Once again in 1992 it was a BMW that won the Championship (competitive drivers including Championship winner Tim Harvey used a suitably tuned new-shape 318iS instead of the obsolete M3): Harvey won six of the 15 races, while all the other plaudits went to Vauxhall Cavaliers (five victories) and Toyota Carinas (four victories). Nissan continued to develop the Primera GT with Janspeed, while the first Mazda 323s and Peugeot 405 Mi16s also appeared.

In personal terms, the big controversy was that 1991 Champion Will Hoy had joined Andy Rouse in a Toyota, but it soon became clear that the two drivers did not get on. Hoy so nearly won the Championship (with two wins and five seconds), but would not drive for Rouse again.

As the technology war hotted up, the next big changes came in 1993. Not only did Ford return, by hiring Andy Rouse to develop the all-new Mondeo, but BMW ran a fully-fledged 'works' team using four-door 318i models, Renault chimed in with two rather evil-handling 19 models, the Nissan Primera GTs and new-shape Toyota Carinas began to look competitive, and there was also Patrick Watts in a Mazda Xedos 6 for variety.

Most pundits agreed that the Mondeo was the real revelation in 1993. Late in arriving – early in the year Andy Rouse had built a V6-engined rear-wheel-drive car but found it slow in testing, and eventually converted the design to a more conventional front-wheel-drive layout – Paul Radisich finished third on its second outing, then won three times and finished second twice before the end of the year. Not only that, but Paul then went off to Monza in the same car, and won the FIA World Touring Car Challenge.

Even so, it was BMW's Motorsport Team that won the Championship, with some ease. 'Smoking Jo' Winkelhock won five races, while his team-mate Steve Soper won three times – but it was fascinating to see that neither could really figure after the Mondeo started winning.

In just two seasons, therefore, the overall picture had changed completely – from 1991 when BMW and Vauxhall ruled the roost, to 1993 when no fewer than six different brands figured in the Championship 'Top Ten', and nine different makes of car competed at one time or another.

Then, in 1994, there was another step change – not only in engineering, but in publicity and marketing interest. Not only did Renault have a major re-think, and bring in a pair of beautifully-prepared Lagunas – which were faster and much more effective than the 19s had ever been – but Volvo confounded everyone by hiring Tom Walkinshaw's TWR organisation to run a pair of 850SE estate cars. That's right: estate cars. For sure there was an element of hype here, but the fact, apparently, was that the wagon-back cars were no less aerodynamic than the rather boxy saloons on which they were based.

The big controversy, however, was over Alfa Romeo's special homologation of the '155 Silverstone', which had special down-force-enhancing front and rear spoilers. Other teams thought this to be sharp practice, protested and got their way, so by mid-season these add-ons were banned. Even so, the combination of driver Gabriele Tarquini, a very strong engine and a good chassis saw the Italians win nine races and lift the Championship very comfortably from Alain Menu's Renault Laguna and Paul Radisich's Ford Mondeo.

Technically, too, this was a year in which BMW, Ford, Peugeot, Renault, Toyota, Vauxhall – and Volvo – were all prominent, all with 300bhp-plus, all running at minimum weights, and all making contact with their rivals from time to time. From mid-season regulations defining the minimum weight gap between front-drive and rear-drive cars was reduced by 50kg, to give BMW more of a chance. Winkelhock won the next race and BMW took four more before the season's end – but too late to challenge Alfa Romeo.

The Volvo programme, to be honest, was all froth and few results – weight was always a problem, neither car ever finished higher than fifth, and was usually well below tenth place – so for 1995 the team opted to run saloons instead, which was a definite step forward. A definite step forward, indeed, this being a year when the 850 saloons won six races and many podium positions. Even so, the stars of the season were the rejuvenated Vauxhall Cavaliers (John Cleland became Champion, six years on from his Astra success of 1989), and the Renault Lagunas (a team run by the Williams F1 operation took ten wins, which urged Menu to second overall). Hampered by heavy V6 engines, and front tyres which often went off under pressure, Paul Radisich's Mondeo won only once, BMW 318s and Alfa Romeos (even with Gabriele Tarquini driving) were way off the pace.

In 1996 the big talking point was the rampant success of the four-wheel-drive Audi A4s, which had previously performed so well in Europe, but had not bothered with British racing. Even though they started the season with a compulsory minimum weight handicap of 65kg compared with the front-wheel-drive cars (another 30kg was arbitrarily imposed by TOCA officials from mid-season), it might have been even more decisive.

Frank Biela swept into the BTCC like a true champion, finishing all but two of the 26 races, winning eight times and taking second eight times more. Not even victories from other rejuvenated teams – four for Menu's Renault Laguna, four for Winkelhock's Schnitzer-prepared BMW 320i, four for Rickard Rydell's Vovo 850, and a creditable three for David Leslie's Honda Accord – could upset that progress. Ford, Vauxhall, Peugeot and a semi-works Nissan effort from Andy Rouse struggled to match up to that.

By 1997, racing in the Super Touring category was at its height. The cars were technically more sophisticated than ever, the racing was ultra-close, and the spectacle made them real crowd-pleasers. Not for nothing did *Autosport*'s annual survey begin with: 'Brilliant, unpredictable racing. A host of different winners. A championship whose destiny remained in doubt right up until the closing stages of the season...'

Familiar shapes made most of the running, and took most of the trophies – but not in the same order as before. Audi could not repeat its 1996 successes – the latest draconian regulations meant that the four-wheel-drive A4s had to carry too much weight, and the Germans took time to develop a simpler front-wheel-drive version – so seven race victories were not quite enough. TWR's Volvos – smaller S40s instead of the heavier old 850s – were quicker than ever, but it was Alain Menu's astonishingly fast and reliable Renault Laguna that made most of the headlines. Not only did Menu win twelve of the 24 races, but he also annexed nine other podium positions; he won the series by 110 points (281 from the Biela/Audi A4's 171). There could be no arguing against that.

Other teams suffered big reverses. Even though Prodrive took up the Honda challenge, they could only win twice, while Ford's Mondeos, Vauxhall's Vectras and Peugeot's 406s all struggled even to be credible. And of BMW... there was no sign.

Disillusion then set in among drivers, teams and (for they had to pay the bills) manufacturers in 1998, where only TWR's Volvos, Ray Mallock's Nissan Primeras, Prodrive's Honda Accords and Williams's Renault Lagunas were truly on the pace. Super Tourer pioneers like Vauxhall, BMW, and Ford didn't figure at all, and several made it clear that they would soon withdraw because it was all getting too costly for them.

TWR, though, proved yet again that they might be a high-maintenance team, but that they could eventually deliver success. Although the Swedish ace, Rickard Rydell, only won five of the 26 races, he also chalked up 12 other podium finishes, and was a model of consistency. Even so, if points scoring had only begun in the second half of the season, all honours would have gone to Anthony Reid's Nissan Primera, which won six times while Rydell won just twice.

Ford hired Prodrive to transform their Mondeos for 1999, while Nissan asked Ray Mallock to do the same with its Primeras. It worked for the Japanese (and Frenchman Laurent Aiello), but not for Ford, who would have to wait until 2000. In the meantime, TWR's Volvos and Williams's Renaults were as competitive as ever, though once again Vauxhall (with Vectras run by Triple Eight) were a big disappointment. In the end it was Aiello/Nissan who won from his so-called 'team-mate' David Leslie (there was no love lost between the two).

Abruptly, though, the Super Touring balloon seemed to deflate, for although the 2000-vintage saloons were even faster than before, there were so very few of them. In sporting terms, the miracle was the turnaround in Prodrive's Mondeos, which had been such a disappointment in 1999 but completely dominated the scene in 2000.

However, the mid-1990s days of nine factory-backed teams battling for the title were now over, for in 2000 there were only three teams in the chase – Ford, Honda and Vauxhall. The Mondeos won 12 of the 24 races, and each driver won races, but it was Menu, with seven successes, who won the trophy at the end of the year.

If nothing else, Prodrive proved that an assiduous study of the rule book helped a lot, for their cars seemed very different from previous-generation Mondeos, and the team clashed with the eligibility scrutineers on several occasions. Few, however, seem to excel in sport by being 'Mr Nice Guy' for long, Prodrive was determined to win, and this surely proved the point.

Whatever, at the end of the year, not only were the established organisers, TOCA, told that they were to lose the franchise in 2002, but that for 2001 an entirely different saloon car race formula would take over. Happy that they could do no more, therefore, Ford retired the Mondeos, while Vauxhall (who had lobbied for a change of regulations) prepared for a big come-back. For the 2000s, the cars would be slower and simpler – but would the racing still be as vivid?

At the height of the Super Touring Car period, there was great variety – here, in 1996, John Cleland's Vauxhall Vectra leads two BMWs, from an Audi A4, on the National Circuit at Silverstone.

Audi's four-wheel-drive A4s came into the BTCC in 1996, and immediately became race winners. Cars driven by Frank Biela and (here) John Bintcliffe were just as fast, and had better traction, than all the other Super Touring cars.

By 1997 Vauxhall's medium-sized Super Tourers had reached their peak, with no more power to come. These were the smart Vectras, which could not quite match the pace of the latest Renault Lagunas and Honda Accords.

John Cleland won the BTCC in 1995 in a Vauxhall Cavalier, then for 1996 changed over to the new model Vectra.

⬆ Even though they were theoretically team-mates, in the mid-1990s drivers in identical cars always tried to out-do each other. Two Vectras, nose to tail here, with James Thompson ahead of John Cleland.

↗ Before the start of the 1995 BTCC season, TOCA arranged a photo-shoot of all the cars that would be involved. Running in close formation were a Vauxhall Cavalier, a BMW 318, a Toyota Carina, a Volvo 850, a Renault Laguna and a Peugeot 405, with other cars hidden from view.

➡ In 1991 and 1992, Andy Rouse developed the Toyota Carina into a race-winning BTCC car – in 1991 he finished third overall in the series.

⬆ In 1992 the two Toyota Carinas were always in contention for the BTCC with Andy Rouse (ahead) and Will Hoy winning several races. Hoy finished second in the Championship.

↗ BMW 3 Series cars were always competitive in the BTCC, for their preparation – and their engines – were among the finest in the business. This was Steve Soper's 318is in 1994, the second year of the *Auto Trader* sponsored BTCCs.

➡ Volvo's 850 saloons might have looked boxy in the BTCC in 1995, but Rickard Rydell and Tim Harvey finished third and fifth, notching up several victories along the way.

→ Britain's leading role in worldwide Touring Car racing was demonstrated in 1994 when the second of the short-lived Touring Car World Cup events was held at Donington Park. Ford's Paul Radisich, leading here, won the race, as he had done a year earlier at Monza in Italy.

Pembrey in 1993, with Ford Mondeo, Mazda Xedos, Renault 19, Peugeot 405, Vauxhall Cavalier and BMW 3 Series all in contention.

Having missed out in 1991 and 1992, Ford came back into the BTCC in 1993, with the first of the Mondeos, as prepared by Andy Rouse. The Mondeo won on only its third outing, and was the pace-setter for two seasons.

If teams and manufacturers could raise the budgets, Super Touring Car regulations allowed most 2-litre cars to be competitive in the BTCC – here, at Brands Hatch, are a Ford Mondeo, Peugeot 405 and BMW 318is all within feet of each other.

⬆ This posed-for-TOCA picture of BTCC cars ready for the 1997 season including Ford Mondeo, Audi A4, Vauxhall Vectra, Peugeot 406, Renault Laguna, Nissan Primera and Honda Accord all ready to go motor racing.

↗ Paul Radisich was one of the stars of BTCC racing in the mid-1990s. Here, in his 1993 example, he is on his way to another victory at Silverstone.

➡ Prodrive took over the running of the 'works' Ford Mondeos in 1999. and though they only won one race, their potential was obvious – they would dominate in 2000.

PAGES 156–157 Prodrive usually entered three brightly-hued Mondeos in the 2000 BTCC series, these cars clearly having the legs on any other competitors, including the hard-driven Vauxhall Vectras which came so close, so often.

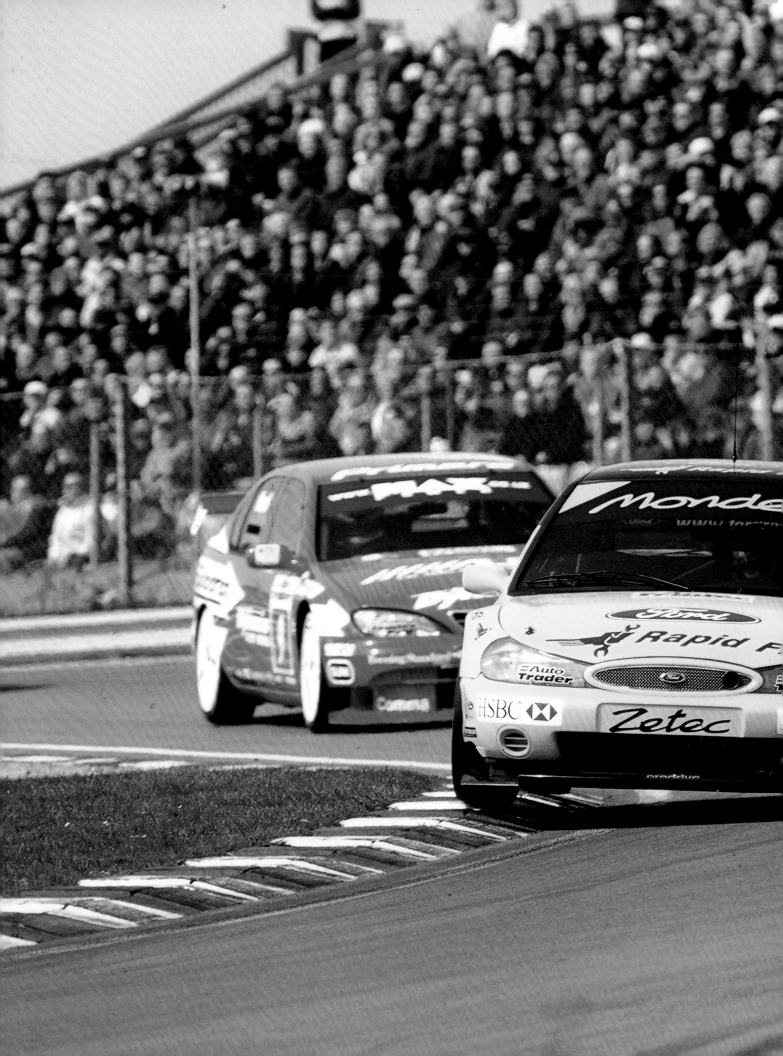

⬆ The Master – Andy Rouse – was 'Mr BTCC' for two decades, winning the Championship in 1975, 1983, 1984 and 1985, and winning more races than any other individual. He engineered his own cars, including the Sierra RS500 Cosworths, Toyota Carinas and Ford Mondeos of the 1990s. This was the interior of his Mondeo in 1994.

⬉ Prodrive's work on the Mondeos throughout 1999 would bring big rewards a year later, when they took first, second and third overall in the Championship, with Alain Menu taking the drivers' title.

⬅ The Renault Lagunas were always competitive. In 1996 Will Hoy (this car – third at Brands Hatch) and Alain Menu drove the cars.

⬆ Jo Winkelhock drove his heart out in BMWs in the mid-1990s, but these rear-drive cars could not match their front-wheel-drive opposition in this period.

◤ When Audi sent four-wheel-drive A4s to tackle the BTCC In 1996, with Frank Biela as their lead driver, it was immediately a winning combination.

⬅ For Andy Rouse, the preparation of a works-supported Nissan Primera in 1996 was a quiet swansong to a glittering career.

⬆ A no-contact sport? Well, yes, but... In 1991 this Cavalier couldn't get much closer to the Labatt's BMW.

⬅ Ultra-close racing as the cars swoop down from Druids Hill hairpin at Brands Hatch in June 1996, with Alain Menu's Renault Laguna in the lead.

Brands Hatch in June 1996, with Frank Biela's Audi just ahead of Rickard Rydell's Volvo 850, fighting for second place.

Kelvin Burt (Volvo 850) just ahead of Jo Winkelhock (BMW 320i) in a 1996 race at Silverstone.

Although the Alfa Romeo 155 had been dominant in 1994, by 1995 other teams had caught up, which made this effort, with Derek Warwick or Giampiero Simoni more difficult to sustain.

⬆ John Cleland's Vectra, in 1997, a year in which the Vauxhalls struggled to stay on terms with the new-generation of Super Tourers.

⬅ Vauxhall, Volvo, Audi, Volvo – BTCC racing was often as close as this in the mid-1990s.

⬆ Strictly anonymous Vauxhall Cavalier of David Leslie (when did you last see a white racing car?) being harried by the Listerine BMW

◤ Vauxhall Vectra versus Peugeot 406 – neither being race winning cars in 1997, though competition was always close.

◀ Before Matt Neal became a regular winner in the 2000s, he sprung to fame in his own cars, sponsored by the family firm. This was his Ford Mondeo in the late 1990s.

← 1991, with John Cleland's Cavalier just ahead of a phalanx of BMWs – Will Hoy, Steve Soper and Ray Bellm were all successful BMW pilots in that year, with Hoy just beating Cleland for the overall title.

↙ John Cleland + Vauxhall Cavalier was a potent combination for years; this was 1992 when the Scottish driver took third place in the Championship.

↓ Yvan Muller was a Vauxhall Vectra star driver in 1999, and in this shot he is being harried by James Thompson's Honda Accord.

⬆ Gabriele Tarquini won the 1994 BTCC in a very special Alfa Romeo, and in 1997 finished sixth in this Prodrive-prepared Honda Accord. James Thompson's sister car is right behind.

↗ Among many to drive the Honda Accord in the Super Touring years was Dutchman Peter Kox in 1998. But he could not match the performances of team-mate James Thompson, who finished third in that year's championship.

➡ By 1997 the 2-litre Honda Accords, as prepared by Prodrive and driven here by James Thompson, were extremely competitive, but found it difficult to compete against the really big spending teams.

At the height of the expensive technology boom in Super Touring Car motor sport, James Thompson drove this Honda Accord into fifth place in the 1997 series.

⬆ In 1992 BMW chose to run much-modified 318is two-door saloons. Alain Menu, supported by BMW Finance, was still learning his trade.

➡ Throughout the 1990s, BMW invariably built the best handling cars, but could not always keep up with the more nimble front-wheel-drive cars. This was 1992, with BTCC rookie Alain Menu at Snetterton.

⬆ Gabriele Tarquini set new standards when he raced the Alfa Romeo 155 in the UK in 1994. A 'tight' front differential meant that he could jump over kerbs without losing any time.

◤ The Alfa Romeos appeared in 1994 and 1995, with Gabriele Tarquini winning the Championship convincingly in 1994.

◀ Side by side, and meaning to stay ahead of their competition, are the two Alfa Romeo 155s which set the pace in BTCC racing in 1994.

↑Although the Alfa 155 looked somewhat narrow and upright in the mid-1990s, it had a very powerful engine, and was superbly prepared.

←Having won the 1994 BTCC in his Alfa Romeo 155, Gabriele Tarquini deserved to carry Competition Number 1 in 1995.

➡This was what BTCC racing was all about in the mid-1990s. Here, at Donington Park, Alfa Romeo leads Toyota, from Peugeot, and a pack of competing makes.

↑ Parking space, anyone? This first-lap traffic jam at Donington Park includes Honda, Alfa Romeo, Peugeot and Ford Mondeo, all within a few cars' lengths.

↗ In 1991 BMW were better-prepared, and better-experienced that any other make of car in the BTCC. Steve Soper drove a 2-litre BMW M3 throughout the season, and finished fourth in the series.

→ Honda Accord (Gabriele Tarquini) versus Renault Laguna (Alain Menu) in 1997. That was a season in which Renault definitely had the edge.

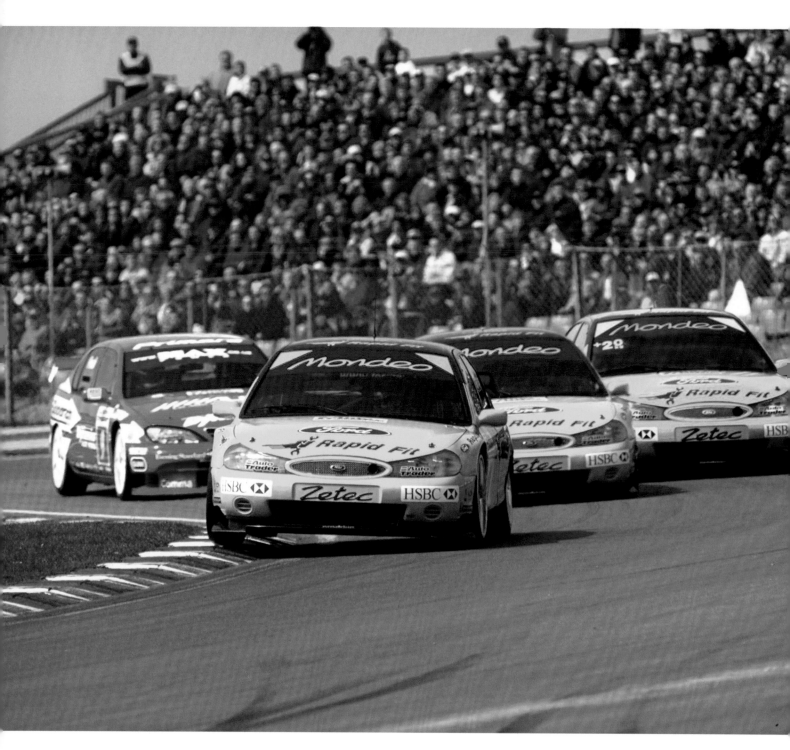

⬆ Mondeos raced in the BTCC from 1993 to 2000, an eight year career. Sometimes let down by their heavy V6 engines, sometimes by tyres, but in 2000 the Prodrive preparation, and the Michelin tyre supplies, made them formidable race winners. They won many races – and there were no team orders.

↗ Maybe you go faster if there is no friction to slow down the tyres. This was Anthony Reid enjoying himself in 2000.

➡ Alain Menu celebrating victory in the 2000 BTCC – his career had blossomed in this series, and the Ford Mondeos that he drove were coming to the end of their lives.

BTCC cars rarely raced in the dark, but at Silverstone in 2000 there was one truly exciting night-time event. This is the compulsory pit stop for tyre changes.

⬆ During the Super Touring Car era, crowds grew to immense proportions, and the pit-lane autograph sessions were always a huge success.

◤ Vauxhall man John Cleland was a constant factor throughout the Super Touring era, and a crowd favourite.

◀ Pit stop time at Donnington Park, for one of the 'works' Vauxhalls.

⬆ Volvo's TWR-built 850 estate cars might have looked unwieldy when they appeared in 1994, but their star drivers – Rickard Rydell and Jan Lammers – took them very seriously indeed.

➡ Although they looked large and boxy, Volvo's 850 estate cars were nimble, and amazingly competitive. This was Jan Lammers, in 1994.

⬆ Rickard Rydell won the Championship in 1998.

⬅ To follow the big 850s, Volvo campaigned the smaller S40s in the late 1990s. Rickard Rydell won the Series in 1998, backed up by team-mate Gianni Morbidelli.

For 2001 it was all change, with an entirely new Touring Car formula, and entirely new racing cars, taking part in the BTCC, for soaring costs had finally forced all but two or three makers out of the sport. In the upheaval that ensued, the 2-litre engined Super Touring Cars, which had been so wonderful to watch in the 1990s, were all outlawed. Not a single car that had competed in 2000 could compete in 2001, for new regulations cut sharply back on technical innovation and specialisation. Although several manufacturers had lobbied for such changes, only one – Vauxhall – took advantage of them at first.

Famous cars like the Super Touring Ford Mondeos, Audi A4s, Vauxhall Vectras, Renault Lagunas, Volvo S40s, Honda Accords and Nissan Primeras were all swept peremptorily aside, and replaced by much less exciting machinery. Because Vauxhall had planned for this, and fine-tuned the latest Astra Coupés well in advance, it would be years before they could be matched. In later years, indeed, Vauxhall's motorsport boss, Mike Nicholson, admitted that they were never flat out in the first one or two seasons, and that some type of team orders were often applied.

For 2001, the new cars were essentially built to a warmed-over Super Production car specification (engines produced only about 270bhp, compared with about 310–320bhp for the last of the Super Tourers), though with sequential transmissions and outrageous aerodynamic body modifications allowed. Not only that, but a series of universal 'control' parts – tyres by B.F. Goodrich, suspension, transmission and brake installations – all helped to keep costs in check, especially as these could so easily be inspected and verified by vigilant scrutineers. The AA, too, came in as a short-lived new sponsor.

Even though series boss Alan Gow stood down, to be replaced by Richard West, the Gow-innovation of penalising regular winners by 'success ballast' was continued. In 2001, the Vauxhalls were so dominant that they were soon carrying 60kg as a matter of course, and before long BTCC officials soon added an extra 30kg on top of that; no matter, though it was reckoned to cost at least one second every lap, the Astras were so dominant that they continued to win, anyway.

Concerning 2001, there is little to tell that was not about Vauxhall. Four 'works' cars from Triple Eight won 25 of the 26 races (Anthony Reid's MG ZS won once on a soaking Brands Hatch track later in the season) with ten victories going to Yvan Muller and eight to Jason Plato. Bad blood erupted between the two, in the form of much bumping and barging, but the spectators seemed to lap this up.

After that, the Peugeot 406 Coupés, several Alfa 147s and a couple of Lexus IS200s were all make-weights. The only promise was that the MG ZSs might cause trouble in 2002 if development continued, and the budget was forthcoming. The Production Class, for Super Production (less powerful, less specialised) cars helped produce healthier grid sizes, but was otherwise irrelevant. None of the cars, and almost none of the drivers who competed, ever graduated to better and more specialised tin-top racing.

After which everyone sat back and wondered if things would get better, faster and more competitive in 2002? Not really – the same, but a bit different, though Green Flag arrived to make some more noise, as a new title sponsor. Vauxhalls still dominated, but this time there were 'only' three

of them in the top positions. James Thompson and Yvan Muller fought it out, apparently without team orders, and yet again it was the unfortunate Muller who had to settle for being runner-up. Thompson was delighted to win the series for the first time – and he, of course, would later go on to even higher things.

The MG ZSs (supported by the cash-strapped MG-Rover factory, but with race cars prepared by West Surrey Racing), which had promised so much in 2001, won three races in 2002, while the new high-revving Honda Civic Type-R won two races too, but the biggest talking point was that Proton (of all people) entered cars, which were often surprisingly competitive. The Peugeots – now 'ex-works' cars – didn't improve, and nothing else turned up to challenge the Vauxhalls, which won 15 races. Matt Neal's car was almost, if not quite, a match for the two 'official' works cars, this forceful driver promising much for future years.

By this time, the BTCC was becoming thoroughly predictable. Spectators moaned that the latest cars were not quick enough, and not exciting enough (though they could not complain about the close racing), the drivers regularly moaned about the way that 'success ballast' negated some of their brilliance, and team bosses kept on whinging that the use of 'control' tyres, and components, made their engineers' jobs difficult.

So, for 2003, would it all be different? For sure there were changes – Dunlop instead of B.F. Goodrich tyres, Alan Gow back in charge of the series, and a promise that this would indeed be the last year for the rather dull 'Production class' – but at the front of the field it was much the same as before. Vauxhall Astra Coupés won ten of the twenty races, the MG ZSs were not as successful as the 'British-by-Gad' fanatics had hoped they would be, and the much-hyped Honda Civic Type-R brigade didn't quite make the breakthrough that its sponsors had hoped.

Vauxhall, therefore, won the series for the third successive time and this time, to the great joy of his many fans, it was Yvan Muller who finally stood on the top step at the end of the year, ahead of James Thompson – which was a slick reversal of what had occurred in 2002. Vauxhall too were pleased to know that their (French) Sodemo-built engines were much more reliable than before.

The result was that Muller won six times, finished second six times, and third five times, which was amazingly consistent; his lowest finishing position was fifth overall, a record which runner up Thompson (four victories, six second places) would have loved to emulate. Success ballast or no success ballast (and the Astras always seemed to be competitive with this weight around their necks), the Vauxhalls set almost every pace at almost every circuit.

As before, too, Matt Neal took third in the Championship, but this time he was driving the always-improving works-backed Honda Civic Type-R instead of a quasi-works Vauxhall Astra Coupé. Like Muller, he won six races, but somehow wasn't as consistent as he would have liked.

And what about the MG ZSs? Looking very purposeful in their green-and-black livery, and with Anthony Reid as team leader, they threatened to do much better than they actually did. Each team driver – Reid, Warren Hughes and Colin Turkington – won one race each, but there were too many retirements, and in a straight fight they could rarely match the Vauxhalls.

Alan Gow, a thrusting marketing man to his fingertips, set about crafting a new image for the BTCC, by arranging for only ten race weekends in 2004, but with three separate races (two sprint and one 'endurance') at each location. To quote what one-time Brands Hatch supreme John Webb once said, 'I'm not sure about long races. The public just love starts and finishes...' This worked, up to a point, but it could not disguise the lack of performance compared with the 1990s. Competition – sometimes even between driver and driver in the same team – was always fierce, and quite a bit of bumping and barging took place throughout the year.

Although the statistics show that ten drivers in four different types of car would win races in 2004, they also hid the fact that 'show-business' in the form of weight and grid position handicapping sometimes got in the way of pure motorsport. By this time, too, the public was beginning to suffer a little from 'Vauxhall-fatigue', though SEAT (especially with Jason Plato back in the series) were always competitive. Even though the Astras 'only' won eleven of the season's thirty races, and SEAT won nine times, the 'works' Astra Coupés were so competitive, and so consistent, that the Championship battle was always between Vauxhall drivers James Thompson and Yvan Muller, with Plato a rather distant third. Vauxhall dominated the Manufacturers' contest too.

As in the Sierra RS500 Cosworth era of the late 1980s, there was only so much that the public could take without the yawning setting in, though the situation had not quite got that far. In this case Anthony Reid (MG ZS) and Matt Neal (Honda Civic Type-R) won three races each, and there seemed to be more variety in the line up. Though the two Astras stood at the top of the table, the next Astra was tenth, and was beaten by MG, Honda, and SEAT.

Even so, the BTCC was no longer providing pure motor racing. As with NASCAR racing in the USA, series gauleiter Alan Gow tried, at all times, to ensure close racing which would enhance the must-vaunted TV coverage. Not only was the 'success ballast' system still applied ruthlessly, but partially-reversed starting grids sometime made for very close racing too.

Gow's decision to allow FIA Super 2000 cars (as raced in Europe) to compete, helped bring SEAT into the series, but the S2000 cars had to be given considerably lower weight limits to allow them to be competitive: reduced by 50kg in mid-season, this was soon seen to be unfair, and reduced to 25kg later in the year. The strategy of partially-reversing grids from one sprint race to the next was always controversial, though in the end resourceful team managers learned how to cope with it all.

In September, at the end of the season, and in spite of all the controversy, it still looked as if the best drivers had won, and the best cars had come out on top. In some ways, though, none of this could hide the fact that there seemed only to be ten competitive machines, and the rest of the field, perhaps ten or fifteen more machines, were makeweights.

The fact, though, was that this was beginning to be a formula in which the same drivers were dominant for year after year. Starting in 2001, it seemed, if you were James Thompson, Yvan Muller, Matt Neal, Anthony Reid and Jason Plato, you were always likely to be a top five contender. So, what would happen in 2005?

The answer, unhappily, was that the BTCC then had a rather fallow year – just one, but enough to worry its backers. As *Autosport*'s annual review pointed out: 'A dozen cars, no matter how creatively lined up on the grid, is rarely an impressive sight, yet that's precisely what the British Touring Car Championship served up for its season-opener... By the end of the season the BTCC had expanded to a respectable 18 cars, produced nine race winners and probably the most popular champion in its history. So how will Matt Neal's title year be remembered?'

This summed up admirably, for Neal won six of the 30 races, and was a points scorer in every one. No-one, not even Neal, denied that his driving could be very robust at times, but he had the character to pace himself throughout the season. In general, of course, this was one of the roughest of seasons, for there was a good deal – far too much, really – of body contact in most races.

It was a season in which the Honda Integra-RDC9 became the pace setter, when Vauxhall's replacement for the Astra Coupé, the Sport Hatch, was not as effective, and when the Spanish SEATs seemed to be too heavy to be on the pace at all times, for genuine BTCC cars had seen minimum weights reduced by 25kg. Success ballast imposed on subsequent races (up to 45kg at times), reversed grids, and three races per meeting made this a complex Championship to follow.

Some star names – Neal, Plato, Muller – performed as expected, so it was Dan Eaves, acting as support-man for Matt Neal, who surprised everyone. Eaves won five times, Plato three times, and Muller (fighting to overcome the handicap of a new Vauxhall that didn't seem to be as aerodynamically efficient as the old car) won six races, so it was a very competitive year. Pity, though, about all the bumping and barging.

A year later, in 2006, Matt Neal repeated his 2005 success, still emphatically, still comfortably, and still against his main rival Jason Plato, but there were novelties too: SEAT brought along the new Leon, which was more competitive than before; James Thompson returned from competition in Europe to back up Plato in the second of the Spanish cars; and Colin Turkington was amazingly competitive in the MG ZS which had really lacked support since MG-Rover had nose-dived into administration in 2005. Once again the European-spec. S2000 SEAT struggled to keep up with the more favourably specified BTCC cars, but with eight wins for Plato and three for Thompson you might be excused for not knowing this.

The fields, in general, were more full than before – with 29 different drivers, of which 22 scored points, and with grids back up to late-1990s levels. Even so, there was no matching the Halfords'-sponsored Neal – eight wins, and nine other podium finishes – and it was really all over by mid-season. But it was still a very 'physical' business: cynics suggested that it had become akin to high-speed banger racing, and there is no doubt that there was a certain type of spectator who was as interested in the bumps, bangs and race-stopping crashes as in the close racing.

A new era began in 2007, with the BTCC adopting the Super 2000 regulations used in the growing World Touring Car Championship. Vauxhall team boss Ian Harrison complained bitterly at the vagaries of such rules, aware that the rival SEATs had been racing to them for years, but at the end of the season Vauxhall's new Vectra was triumphant in the hands of Fabrizio Giovanardi, setting the BTCC up for its second fifty years of competition.

↑ The combination of Anthony Reid's driving, hugely effective aerodynamic add-ons, and very sure-footed behaviour in the rain, made the WSR-prepared MG ZS a competitive machine in the early 2000s.

↘ Anthony Reid (left) and Warren Hughes were delighted with their MG ZSs in the BTCC of 2002, finishing fourth and sixth in the overall standings. The cars, prepared by West Surrey Racing, won three races in 2002, against the overwhelming odds of a fleet of 'works' Vauxhalls. If only a bigger budget had been available, Anthony Reid might have finished even higher in the series.

← Although the MG ZSs were always underfinanced in the early 2000s, because of MG-Rover's acknowledged problems, Anthony Reid made up for that with spirited driving.

◁ Dominant for much of the time, in very close racing, the two-car Halfords/Honda Integra team of Matt Neal and Gordon Shedden made many headlines in 2006.

↑ SEAT was serious about its BTCC programme in the mid-2000s. This, the latest-style Leon, appeared in 2006, when Jason Plato won several races, and finished second in the Championship.

◥ After years of success with the Honda Integra, the new Super 2000 rules in 2007 saw Matt Neal switch to a new Civic Type-R.

◄ Close racing indeed, with one of the SEATs just ahead of Matt Neal's Honda Integra Type R in the mid-2000s. The cars were often even closer than that!

Why drive around on four wheels when just one might do the job for a second or two. Colin Turkington's MG ZS at Knockhill in 2004.

⬆ Close racing in 2005, with Jason Plato's Seat Toledo Cupra just, but only just, ahead of Yvan Muller's Vauxhall Astra Sport Hatch.

⬈ One twitch from either driver, and some paint will be exchanged. Jason Plato's new-style Leon side-by-side with Tom Chilton's Vauxhall Astra Sport Hatch in 2006.

➡ Nicely presented, the new Halfords-sponsored 2007 Civic Type-R in which Matt Neal (left) defended his 2006 title, with support from team-mate Gordon Shedden.

⬆ Rob Collard raced this MG ZS in the mid-2000s, but struggled to keep up with the all-conquering Vauxhalls and Hondas.

↗ Colin Turkington (MG ZS) finished a fine and plucky third overall in the 2006 BTCC, in a car which had not really developed much in the last two seasons.

➡ Close competition in 2006, with Colin Turkington's MG ZS ahead of two Vauxhall Astras which were celebrating their 100th BTCC Race win, and the sister MG ZS.

⬆ Warren Hughes raced the then-new MG ZS throughout 2002, finishing sixth in the BTCC series.

↗ The rear wing may look extreme, but was strictly according to the new BTCC regulations which came into force in 2001. This was Jason Plato driving one of the dominant Vauxhall Astra Coupés that won so many races in that year.

➡ We're not really racing against each other – team orders and all that – but the spectators love it. Vauxhall Astras at play in 2001.

Never mind the weather! When new BTCC regulations were applied from 2001, the 'works' Vauxhall team was ready, and up and running, ahead of all its rivals. Yvan Muller, Jason Plato and James Thompson often fought for victory between themselves in their Astra Coupés.

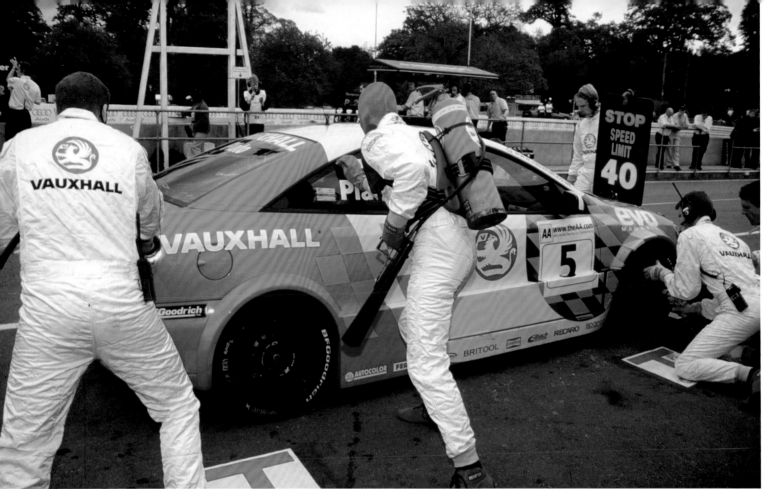

Looks almost like mini-NASCAR time, right? This is an image that the BTCC organisers promoted in the early 2000s. Jason Plato's Vauxhall at Oulton Park in 2001.

Yvan Muller was second to team-mate James Thompson in the 2002 series, both of them driving Vauxhall Astra Coupés. This four-wheel jump was achieved at Brands Hatch.

Yvan Muller claiming the high-jump record for an Astra Coupé, in 2002.

Has Paul O'Neill lost his contact lenses, or is there a more logical explanation?

Wall-to-wall Vauxhalls at the start of a race at Oulton Park in 2002 – with only Hondas breaking up the symmetry.

There was a time, in 2002, when the MG ZSs (green and black) looked as if they might consistently match the massed ranks of Vauxhall – but not for long. Anthony Reid's ZS was fourth in that season.

⬆ At the end of the 2002 season James Thompson (right) and Yvan Muller (left) had finished first and second in the BTCC.

◣ How many BTCC cars can be abreast as they leave the start line at Snetterton? Doesn't bear thinking about, does it?

◀ There was no love lost between Matt Neal and James Thompson in 2002, but they usually kept away from each other in near-identical cars.

⬆ No shortage of cars on the grid for the Brands Hatch qualifier in the 2002 series.

↗ Real variety at the front of a 2002 BTCC race, with James Thompson's Vauxhall ahead of Andy Priaulx's Honda Civic Type R, the Muller Vauxhall and one of the promising MG ZSs.

➡ Matt Neal's car carried Vauxhall's boastful message, even before the end of the 2002 season, which they had completely dominated. Matt himself had finished third overall in that year, but would soon split off, align himself to Honda for future seasons, and soon become outright Champion.

⬆ The BTCC has always attracted huge crowds, who loved getting up close to the drivers, the cars and the teams during the traditional lunchtime pits walkabout.

⬉ Compared with the 1990s, the 2000s breed of BTCC car was much slower than before, but no-one could complain about the closeness of the racing. Vauxhall Astra Coupés battle head-to-head with MG ZS types in this first-corner shot.

⬅ Vauxhall and Honda scrapping together in 2003, that's logical enough – but a Proton in motor racing? Whatever next?

➜ Crowded grid at the start of a 2003 race at Brands Hatch.

⬆ Honda, SEAT, MG and Vauxhall – all of them race-winning contenders in 2004, with 2003 Champion Yvan Muller narrowly in the lead.

⬋ Team mates and rivals James Thompson and Yvan Muller fought over the 2004 series until the very end. This was Muller at Brands Hatch.

⬅ Jason Plato's SEAT Toledo Cupra couldn't get any closer to Yvan Muller's Vauxhall if he tried. Engine overheating would certainly be a problem if this went on for too long.

⬆ Colin Turkington switched from an MG ZS in 2004 to this
Vauxhall Astra Sport Hatch in 2005 – and still finished sixth
overall in the series.

➡ What's a race circuit kerb for if you can't jump it? Yvan
Muller taking the short way at Brands Hatch early in the
2005 season.

With every year that passed, BTCC competition got even closer, and much paint, not to mention a few panel scrapes, were exchanged. Here, Fabrizio Giovanardi's Vauxhall is only inches ahead of one of the new-generation Seat Leons, on the hairpin before the start/finish line at Knockhill in 2006.

It wasn't always glamorous – Vauxhall qualifying in the rain and mist at Knockhill in 2006, with Tom Chilton's car ready to go out on to the track.

This wide-angle lens shot makes Giovanardi's 2007 Vectra look bent, but we're sure Fabrizio would have noticed if it was.

➡ Potential mayhem as the entire 23-car BTCC field, all of them in competitive 2-litre cars, force their way into the first corner at Rockingham in 2007. Guess what – as in most of the 2000s, a Vauxhall was in the lead...

1958

BRSCC Saloon Car Championship

1	Jack Sears (Austin A105 Westminster)	48
2	Tommy Sopwith (Jaguar 3.4)	48
3	John Sprinzel (Austin A35)	47
4	G.C. 'Doc' Shepherd (Austin A35)	41
5	Alan Foster (MG Magnette ZB)	40
6	Jeff Uren (Ford Zephyr)	36

Classes:

Up to 1,200cc	John Sprinzel (Austin A35)
1,201 to 1,600cc	Alan Foster (MG Magnette)
1,601cc to 2,700cc	Jack Sears (Austin A105 Westminster)
Over 2,700cc	Tommy Sopwith (Jaguar 3.4)

1959

BRSCC Saloon car Championship

1	Jeff Uren (Ford Zephyr)	46
2	G.C. 'Doc' Shepherd (Austin A40)	42
3	Les Leston (Riley 1.5)	38
4	Len Adams (Austin A35)	34
5	Bill Blydenstein (Borgward Isabella TS)	33
6	G.H.Williamson (Austin A40)	26

Classes:

Up to 1,300cc	Len Adams (Austin A35)
1,301cc to 1,600cc	Les Leston (Riley 1.5)
1,601cc to 2,600cc	Jeff Uren (Ford Zephyr)

1960

**BRSCC SupaTura Championship
(Limited to Up-to-1-litre cars)**

1	G.C. 'Doc' Shepherd (Austin A40)	48
2	J. Young (Ford Anglia 105E)	30
3	E. Lewis (Austin A40)	13
4=	J. Aley (Austin A35)	
	A. Hedges (Austin A40)	6
6	B. Whitaker (Austin A35)	4

1961

BRSCC Saloon Car Championship

1	Sir John Whitmore (BMC Mini-Minor)	53
2	Mike Parkes (Jaguar 3.8 Mk II)	44
3	Alan Hutcheson (Riley 1.5)	42
4	Bill Blydenstein (Borgward Isabella TS)	42
5	Roy Salvadori (Jaguar 3.8 Mk II)	37
6	Graham Hill (Jaguar 3.8 Mk II)	28

Classes:

Up to 1,000cc	Sir John Whitmore (BMC Mini-Minor)
1,001cc to 2,000cc	Alan Hutcheson (Riley 1.5)
2,001cc to 3,000cc	Chris Kerrison (Jaguar 2.4)
Over 3,000cc	Mike Parkes (Jaguar 3.8 Mk I)

1962

BRSCC Saloon Car Championship

1	John Love (BMC Mini-Cooper)	52
2	Peter Harper (Sunbeam Rapier)	49
3	Jack Sears (Jaguar 3.8 Mk II)	38
4	Graham Hill (Jaguar 3.8 Mk II)	37
5=	Mike Parkes (Jaguar 3.8 Mk II)	32
	Peter Jopp (Sunbeam Rapier)	32

Classes:

Up to 1,000cc	John Love (BMC Mini-Cooper)
1,001cc to 2,000cc	Peter Harper (Sunbeam Rapier)
2,001cc to 3,000cc	David Haynes (Ford Zephyr 6)
Over 3,000cc	Jack Sears (Jaguar 3.8 Mk II)

1963

BRSCC British Saloon Car Championship

1	Jack Sears (Ford Cortina GT, Ford Lotus-Cortina, Ford Galaxie)	71
2	John Whitmore (BMC Mini-Cooper and Mini-Cooper 1071S)	69
3	Graham Hill (Ford Galaxie and Jaguar 3.8 Mk II)	49
4	Roy Salvadori (Ford Galaxie and Jaguar 3.8 Mk II)	38
5	Jimmy Blumer (Ford Cortina GT)	33
6	Paddy Hopkirk (BMC Mini-Cooper and Mini-Cooper 1071S)	30

Classes:

Up to 1,300cc	Sir John Whitmore (Mini-Cooper and Mini-Cooper 1071S)
1,301cc to 2,000cc	Jack Sears (Ford Cortina GT and Ford Cortina-Lotus)
2,001cc to 3,000cc	Alan Mann (Ford Zodiac Mk III)
Over 3,000cc	Graham Hill (Jaguar 3.9 Mk II)

1964

BRSCC British Saloon Car Championship

1	Jim Clark (Ford Lotus-Cortina)	48
2	John Fitzpatrick (BMC Mini-Cooper 1275S)	38
3	Mike Young (Ford Anglia 1200)	30
4	Chris McLaren (Jaguar 3.8 Mk II)	26
5=	Sir Gawaine Baillie (Ford Galaxie 7.0-litre)	24
	Peter Arundell (Ford Lotus-Cortina)	24
	Bob Olthoff (Ford Lotus-Cortina)	24

Classes:

Up to 1,300cc	John Fitzpatrick (Mini-Cooper 1275S)
1,301cc to 2,000cc	Jim Clark (Ford Lotus-Cortina)
2,001cc to 5,000cc	Chris McLaren (Jaguar 3.8 Mk II)
Over 5,000cc	Sir Gawaine Baillie (Ford Galaxie 7.0-litre)

1965

BRSCC British Saloon Car Championship

1	Roy Pierpoint (Ford Mustang)	60
2	Warwick Banks (BMC Mini-Cooper S)	48
3	John Rhodes (BMC Mini-Cooper S)	40
4	Jack Sears (Ford Lotus-Cortina)	38
5	Frank Gardner (Ford Lotus-Cortina)	34
6	Sir Gawaine Baillie (Ford Mustang)	32
7	Jim Clark (Ford Lotus-Cortina)	30

Classes;

Up to 1,000cc	Warwick Banks (Mini-Cooper 970S)
1,001cc to 1,300cc	John Rhodes (Mini-Cooper 1275S)
1,301cc to 2,000cc	Jack Sears (Ford Lotus-Cortina)
Over 2,000cc	Roy Pierpoint (Ford Mustang)

1966

RAC British Saloon Car Championship

1	John Fitzpatrick (Ford Anglia 105E)	50
2	John Rhodes (BMC Mini-Cooper S)	50
3	Peter Arundell (Ford Lotus-Cortina)	38
4	Mike Young (Ford Anglia 1200 Super)	
5=	Jim Clark (Ford Lotus-Cortina)	34
	Sir Gawaine Baillie (Ford Falcon)	34

Classes:

Up to 1,000cc	John Fitzpatrick (Ford Anglia 105E)
1,001cc to 1,300cc	John Rhodes (BMC Mini-Cooper 1275S)
1,301cc to 2,000cc	Peter Arundell (Ford Lotus-Cortina)
Over 2,000cc	Sir Gawaine Baillie (Ford Falcon)

1967

RAC British Saloon Car Championship

1	Frank Gardner (Ford Falcon)	70
2	John Fitzpatrick (Ford Anglia 105E)	62
3	John Rhodes (BMC Mini-Cooper S)	58
4=	Jackie Oliver (Ford Mustang)	54
	Bernard Unett (Hillman Imp)	54

Classes:

Up to 1,000cc	John Fitzpatrick (Ford Anglia 105E)
1,001cc to 1,300cc	John Rhodes (BMC Mini-Cooper 1275S)
1,301cc to 2,000cc	Vic Elford (2.0 Porsche 911)
Over 2,000cc	Frank Gardner (Ford Falcon)

1968

RAC British Saloon Car Championship

1	Frank Gardner (Ford Escort Twin-Cam/Lotus-Cortina)	84
2	Brian Muir (Ford Falcon)	58
3=	Brian Robinson (Ford Lotus-Cortina)	50
	John Rhodes (BMC Mini-Cooper S)	50
5	Roy Pierpoint (Ford Falcon)	44
6	John Fitzpatrick (Ford Escort GT)	42

Classes:

Up to 1,000cc	Gordon Spice (Mini-Cooper 970S)
1,001cc to 1,300cc	John Rhodes (Mini-Cooper 1275S)
1,301cc to 2,000cc	Frank Gardner (Ford Cortina-Lotus, and Ford Escort Twin-Cam)
Over 2,000cc	Brian Muir (Ford Falcon)

1969

RAC British Saloon Car Championship

1	Alec Poole (BMC Mini-Cooper 970S)	76
2	Chris Craft (Ford Escort GT)	67
3	Frank Gardner (Ford Escort Twin-Cam supercharged)	58
4	Mike Crabtree (Ford Escort Twin-Cam)	54
5	Gordon Spice (BMC Mini-Cooper S)	46
6	Rob Mason (BMC Mini-Cooper S)	44
7=	John Fitzpatrick (Ford Escort GT)	44
	Lawrie Hickman (Ford Escort 1.0-litre)	44
	Roy Pierpoint (Ford Falcon)	44

Classes:

Up to 1,000cc	Alec Poole (BMC Mini-Cooper 970S)	
1,001cc to 1,300cc	Chris Craft (Ford Escort GT)	
1,301cc to 2,000cc	Mike Crabtree (Ford Escort Twin-Cam)	
Over 2,000cc	Frank Gardner (Ford Escort Twin-Cam supercharged)	

1970

RAC British Saloon Car Championship

1	Bill McGovern (Sunbeam Imp)	72
2	Frank Gardner (Ford 'Boss' Mustang)	68
3=	John Fitzpatrick (Ford Escort GT)	62
	Brian Muir (Chevrolet Camaro Z28)	62
5	Chris Craft (Ford Escort Twin-Cam)	60
6	Gordon Spice (BMC Mini-Cooper 1275S)	48

Classes:

Up to 1,000cc	Bill McGovern (Sunbeam Rallye Imp)	
1,001cc to 1,300c	John Fitzpatrick (Ford Escort GT)	
1,301cc to 2,000cc	Chris Craft (Ford Escort Twin-Cam)	
Over 2,000cc	Frank Gardner (Ford 5.0-litre 'Boss' Mustang)	

1971

RAC British Saloon Car Championship

1	Bill McGovern (Sunbeam Rallye Imp)	80
2	Dave Matthews (Ford Escort GT)	76
3	Brian Muir (Chevrolet Camaro)	74
4	John Fitzpatrick (Ford Escort RS1600)	60
5	Vince Woodman (Ford Escort GT)	58

Classes:

Up to 1,000cc	Bill McGovern (Sunbeam Rallye Imp)	
1,001cc to 1,300cc	Dave Matthews (Ford Escort 1300GT)	
1,301cc to 2,000cc	John Fitzpatrick (Ford Escort RS1600)	
Over 2,000cc	Brian Muir (Chevrolet Camaro Z28)	

1972

RAC Wiggins Teape Paperchase, British Saloon Car Championship

1	Bill McGovern (Sunbeam Imp)	63
2	Dave Matthews (Ford Escort RS1600)	55
3	Frank Gardner (Chevrolet Camaro)	54
4	Jonathan Buncombe (BMC Mini-Cooper S)	48
5=	Brian Muir (Ford Capri RS2600)	28
	Melvyn Adams (Sunbeam Imp)	28

Classes:

Up to 1,000cc	Bill McGovern (Sunbeam Rallye Imp)	
1,001cc to 1,300cc	Jonathan Buncombe (BMC Mini-Cooper 1275S)	
1,300cc to 2,000cc	Dave Matthews (Ford Escort RS1600)	
Over 2,000cc	Frank Gardner (Chevrolet Camaro)	

1973

RAC British Saloon Car Championship

1	Frank Gardner (Chevrolet Camaro)	66
2=	Andy Rouse (Ford Escort RS1600)	
	Peter Hanson (Ford Escort 'RS1300')	45
4	Vince Woodman (Ford Escort 'RS1300')	43
5	Brian Muir (BMW 3.0CSL)	36
6=	Dave Brodie (Ford Escort RS1600)	
	Les Nash (Sunbeam Imp)	33

Classes:

Up to 1,000cc	Les Nash (Sunbeam Imp)	
1,001cc to 1,300cc	Peter Hanson (Ford Escort 'RS1300')	
1,301cc to 2,000cc	Andy Rouse (Ford Escort RS1600)	
Over 2,000cc	Frank Gardner (Chevrolet Camaro 7.0-litre)	

1974

RAC Castrol Anniversary Saloon Car Championship

1	Bernard Unett (Hillman Avenger GT 1600)	69
2	Andy Rouse (Triumph Dolomite Sprint)	67
3	Stuart Graham (Chevrolet Camaro)	64
4	Tom Walkinshaw (Ford Capri 3000GT)	63
5	Peter Hanson (Opel Commodore)	55
6=	Barry Williams (Mazda RX3)	47
	Tony Lanfranchi (BMW 3.0CSi)	47

Classes:

Up to 1,600cc	Bernard Unett (Chrysler Avenger GT)	
1,601cc to 2,500cc	Andy Rouse (Triumph Dolomite Sprint)	
2,501cc to 4,000cc	Tom Walkinshaw (Ford Capri 3000GT)	
Over 4,000cc	Stuart Graham (Chevrolet Camaro)	

1975

RAC Southern Organs British Saloon Car Championship

1=	Andy Rouse (Triumph Dolomite Sprint)**	78
	Win Percy (Toyota Celica GT)	78
	Stuart Graham (Chevrolet Camaro Z28 7.4-litre)	78
4	Richard Lloyd (Chevrolet Camaro Z28 7.4-litre)	65
5	Vince Woodman (Chevrolet Camaro Z28 7.4-litre)	64
6	Bernard Unett (Hillman Avenger GT 1.5-litre)	63

Classes:

Up to 1,600cc	Win Percy (Toyota Celica GT)	
1,601cc to 2,500cc	Andy Rouse (Triumph Dolomite Sprint)	
2,501cc to 4,000cc	Gordon Spice (Ford Capri 3000GT)	
Over 4,000cc	Stuart Graham (Chevrolet Camaro)	

** Andy Rouse won in the tie-break depending on the greatest number of wins.

1976

RAC Keith Prowse British Touring Car Championship

1	Bernard Unett (Chrysler Avenger GT 1300)	90
2	Win Percy (Toyota Celica GT)	81
3=	Gordon Spice (Ford Capri 3000GT)	58
	Gerry Marshall (Vauxhall Magnum Coupé)	58
5	Tom Walkinshaw (Ford Capri 3000GT)	53
6	Barrie Williams (Toyota Celica GT)	51

Classes:

Up to 1,300cc	Bernard Unett (Chrysler Avenger GT)	
1,301cc to 1,600cc	Win Percy (Toyota Celica GT)	
1,601cc to 2,500cc	Gerry Marshall (Vauxhall Magnum Coupé)	
2,501cc to 3,000cc	Gordon Spice (Ford Capri 3000GT)	

1977

RAC Tricentrol British Saloon Car Championship

1	Bernard Unett (Chrysler Avenger GT)	52
2	Tony Dron (Triumph Dolomite Sprint)	51
3	Richard Lloyd (VW Golf GTi)	41
4	Jeff Allam (Vauxhall Magnum Coupé)	31
5=	Gordon Spice (Ford Capri 3000GT)	28
	Richard Longman (BL Mini 1275GT)	28

Classes:

Up to 1,300cc	Bernard Unett (Chrysler Avenger GT 1300)	
1,301cc to 1,600cc	Richard Lloyd (VW Golf GTi)	
1,601cc to 2,300cc	Tony Dron (Triumph Dolomite Sprint)	
Over 2,500cc	Gordon Spice (Ford Capri 3000GT)	

1978

RAC Tricentrol British Saloon Car Championship

1	Richard Longman (BL Mini 1275GT)	100
2	Richard Lloyd (VW Golf GTi)	90
3	Tony Dron (Triumph Dolomite Sprint)	83
4	Gordon Spice (Ford Capri 3-litre)	75
5	Rex Greenslade (Alfa Romeo Alfasud 1.3)	62
6	Win Percy (Toyota Celica GT 1.6)	56

Classes:

Up to 1,300cc	Richard Longman (Mini 1275GT)	
1,301cc to 1,600cc	Richard Lloyd (VW Golf GTi)	
1,601cc to 2,300cc	Tony Dron (Triumph Dolomite Sprint)	
Over 2,300cc	Gordon Spice (Ford Capri 3-litre)	

1979

RAC Tricentrol British Saloon Car Championship

1	Richard Longman (BL Mini 1275GT)	97
2	Tom Walkinshaw (Mazda RX-7)	88
3	Richard Lloyd (VW Golf GTi)	82
4	Gordon Spice (Ford Capri 3-Litre)	75
5	Win Percy (Toyota Celica GT 1.6)	70
6	Rex Greenslade (Triumph Dolomite Sprint)	53

Classes:

Up to 1,300cc	Richard Longman (BL Mini 1275GT)	
1,301cc to 1,600c	Richard Lloyd (VW Golf GTi)	
1,601cc to 2,300cc	Tom Walkinshaw (Mazda RX-7)	
Over 2,300cc	Gordon Spice (Ford Capri 3-litre)	

1980

RAC Tricentrol British Saloon Car Championship

1	Win Percy (Mazda RX-7)	90
2	Alan Curnow (Ford Fiesta 1300S)	73
3	Gordon Spice (Ford Capri 3-litre)	67
4	Andy Rouse (Ford Capri 3-litre)	64
5	Jon Dooley (Alfa Romeo Alfasud 1.3)	58
6	Chris Hodgetts (Toyota Celica GT)	45

Classes:

Up to 1,300cc	Alan Curnow (Ford Fiesta 1300)
1,301cc to 1,600cc	Chris Hodgetts (Toyota Celica GT)
1,601cc to 2,300cc	Win Percy (Mazda RX-7 2.3-litre)
Over 2,300cc	Gordon Spice (Ford Capri 3-litre)

1981

RAC Tricentrol British Saloon Car Championship

1	Win Percy (Mazda RX-7)	78
2	Chris Hodgetts (Toyota Celica 1.6)	74
3	John Dooley (Alfa Romeo Alfasud)	65
4	John Morris (VW Golf GTi)	60
5	Richard Longman (Austin Metro)	58
6	Peter Lovett (Rover 3500 SD1)	52

Classes:

Up to 1,300cc	Jon Dooley (Alfa Romeo Alfasud)
1,301cc to 1,600cc	Chris Hodgetts (Toyota Celica)
1,601cc to 2,500cc	Win Percy (Mazda RX-7)
Over 2,300cc	Peter Lovett (Rover 3500 SD1)

1982

RAC Tricentrol British Saloon Car Championship

1	Win Percy (Toyota Corolla)	90
2	Richard Longman (Austin Metro)	72
3	Steve Soper (Austin Metro)	65
4	Jeff Allam (Rover 3500 SD1)	62
5	Vince Woodman (Ford Capri 3-litre)	59
6	Hamish Irvine (Triumph Dolomite Sprint)	59

Classes:

Up to 1,300cc	Richard Longman (Austin Mini Metro)
1,301cc to 1,600cc	Win Percy (Toyota Corolla)
1,601cc to 2,500cc	Hamish Irvine (Triumph Dolomite Sprint)
Over 2,500cc	Jeff Allam (Rover 3500 SD1)

1983

RAC Trimoco British Saloon Car Championship

1	Andy Rouse (Alfa Romeo GTV6)	61
2	Alan Minshaw (VW Golf GTi)	45
3	Chris Hodgetts (Ford Escort RS1600i)	43
4=	Alan Curnow (Ford Escort RS1600i)	42
	Hamish Irvine (Mazda RX-7)	42
6	Jon Dooley (Alfa Romeo GTV6)	36

Classes:

Up to 1,600cc	Alan Minshaw (VW Golf GTi)
1,601cc to 2,500cc	Andy Rouse (Alfa Romeo GTV6)
Over 2,500cc	Tony Lanfranchi (Opel Monza

Note: The 'works'-sponsored Rover Vitesses (driven by Steve Soper, Peter Lovett and Jeff Allam) won most individual races, but after the end of the Series were disqualified after a long series of protests and RAC MSA tribunal meetings. Austin-Rover eventually 'disassociated' themselves from the Championship. The Rover Vitesse scores, therefore, have been removed from this table. (If the Rovers had remained in place, they would have ranked first (Soper), second (Lovett) and fourth (Jeff Allam) in the Championship.)

1984

RAC Trimoco British Saloon Car Championship

1	Andy Rouse (Rover Vitesse)	77
2	Richard Longman (Ford Escort RS1600i)	74
3=	Graham Goode (Nissan Bluebird Turbo)	50
	Jon Dooley (Alfa Romeo GTV6)	50
5	Chris Hodgetts (Ford Escort RS1600i)	45
6	Phil Dowsett (Alfa Romeo GTV6)	44

Classes:

Up to 1,600cc	Richard Longman (Ford Escort RS1600i)
1,601cc to 2,500cc	Graham Goode (Nissan Bluebird Turbo)
Over 2,500cc	Andy Rouse (Rover Vitesse)

1985

RAC Trimoco British Saloon Car Championship

1	Andy Rouse (Ford Merkur XR4Ti)	86
2	Chris Hodgetts (Ford Escort RS1600i)	76
3	Richard Belcher (Ford Escort RS1600i)	60
4	Dave Brodie (Colt Starion Turbo)	54
5	Alan Curnow (Ford Escort RS1600i)	52
6	Rob Kirby (Alfa Romeo GTV6)	49

Classes:

Up to 1,600cc	Chris Hodgetts (Ford Escort RS1600i)
1,601cc to 2,500cc	Rob Kirby (Alfa Romeo GTV6)
Over 2,500cc	Andy Rouse (Ford Merkur XR4Ti)

1986

RAC British Saloon Car Championship

1	Chris Hodgetts (Toyota Corolla GT)	70
2	Richard Longman (Ford Escort RS Turbo)	64
3	Andy Rouse (Ford Merkur XR4Ti)	57
4	Rob Kirby (Alfa Romeo GTV6/75)	38
5	Mike Newman (BMW 635CSi)	37
6	Pete Hall (Rover Vitesse)	34

Classes:

Up to 1,300cc	Tony Lanfranchi (Vauxhall Nova Sport)
1,301cc to 1,600cc	Chris Hodgetts (Toyota Corolla GT)
1,601cc to 2,500cc	Richard Longman (Ford Escort RS Turbo)
Over 2,500cc	Andy Rouse (Ford Merkur XR4Ti)

1987

RAC Dunlop British Touring Car Championship

1	Chris Hodgetts (Toyota Corolla GT)	84
2	Mark Hales (Ford Escort RS Turbo)	51
3	Jon Dooley (Alfa Romeo 75 Turbo)	47
4=	Tim Harvey (Rover Vitesse)	45
	Geoff Kimber-Smith (Toyota Corolla GT)	45
6	Dennis Leech (Rover Vitesse)	44

Classes:

Up to 1,600cc	Chris Hodgetts (Toyota Corolla GT)
1,601cc to 2,000cc	Colin Pearcy (MG Metro Turbo)
2,001cc to 2,500cc	Mark Hales (Ford Escort RS Turbo)
Over 2,500cc	Tim Harvey (Rover Vitesse)

1988

RAC Dunlop British Touring Car Championship

1	Frank Sytner (BMW M3)	103
2	Phil Dowsett (Toyota Corolla GT)	98
3	Andy Rouse (Ford Sierra RS500 Cosworth)	95
4	Godfrey Hall (BMW M3)	48
5	Mike Smith (BMW M3)	39
6	Jerry Mahony (Ford Sierra RS500 Cosworth)	33

Classes:

Up to 1,600cc	Phil Dowsett (Toyota Corolla GT)
1,601cc to 2,000cc	James Shead (VW Golf GTi)
2,001cc to 2,500cc	Frank Sytner (BMW M3)
Over 2,500cc	Andy Rouse (Ford Sierra RS500 Cosworth)

1989

RAC Esso British Touring Car Championship

1	John Cleland (Vauxhall Astra GTE)	110
2	James Weaver (BMW M3)	109
3	Andy Rouse (Ford Sierra RS500 Cosworth)	78
4	Robb Gravett (Ford Sierra RS500 Cosworth)	74
5	Louise Aitken-Walker (Vauxhall Astra GTE)	72
6	Frank Sytner (BMW M3)	70

Classes:

Up to 1,600cc	Phil Dowsett (Toyota Corolla GT)
1,601cc – 2,000cc	John Cleland (Vauxhall Astra GTE 16v)
2,001cc to 2,500cc	James Weaver (BMW M3)
Over 2,500cc	Andy Rouse (Ford Sierra RS500 Cosworth)

1990

RAC Esso British Touring Car Championship

1	Robb Gravett (Ford Sierra RS500 Cosworth)	207
2	Frank Sytner (BMW M3, 2.0-litre engine)	180
3	Andy Rouse (Ford Sierra RS500 Cosworth)	173
4	Tim Harvey (Ford Sierra RS500 Cosworth)	132
5	John Cleland (Vauxhall Cavalier GSi)	128
6	Jeff Allam (BMW M3, 2.0-litre engine)	124

Classes:

Class A (Group A cars)	Robb Gravett (Ford Sierra RS500 Cosworth)
Class B (Up to 2,000cc)	Frank Sytner (BMW M3, 2.0-litre engine)

1991

RAC Esso British Touring Car Championship

1	Will Hoy (BMW M3)	155
2	John Cleland (Vauxhall Cavalier GSi)	132
3	Andy Rouse (Toyota Carina)	115
4	Steve Soper (BMW M3)	96
5	Ray Bellm (BMW M3)	90
6	Jeff Allam (Vauxhall Cavalier GSi)	80

1992

RAC Esso British Touring Car Championship

1	Tim Harvey (BMW 318iS)	152
2	Will Hoy (Toyota Carina)	149
3	John Cleland (Vauxhall Cavalier)	145
4	Jeff Allam (Vauxhall Cavalier)	137
5	Andy Rouse (Toyota Carina)	128
6	Steve Soper (BMW 318iS)	77

1993

Auto Trader British Touring Car Championship

1	Jo Winkelhock (BMW 318i)	163
2	Steve Soper (BMW 318i)	150
3	Paul Radisich (Ford Mondeo Si)	110
4	John Cleland (Vauxhall Cavalier 16V)	102
5	Julian Bailey (Toyota Carina E)	88
6	Keith Odor (Nissan Primera eGT)	82

1994

Auto Trader British Touring Car Championship

1	Gabriele Tarquini (Alfa Romeo 155 Silverstone)	298
2	Alain Menu (Renault Laguna)	222
3	Paul Radisich (Ford Mondeo Ghia)	206
4	John Cleland (Vauxhall Cavalier 16V)	177
5	Giampiero Simoni (Alfa Romeo 155 Silverstone)	156
6	Joachim Winkelhock (BMW 318i)	147

1995

Auto Trader British Touring Car Championship

1	John Cleland (Vauxhall Cavalier 16V)	348
2	Alain Menu (Renault Laguna)	305
3	Rickard Rydell (Volvo 850)	255
4	Will Hoy (Renault Laguna)	195
5	Tim Harvey (Volvo 850)	176
6	Paul Radisich (Ford Mondeo Ghia)	130

1996

Auto Trader British Touring Car Championship

1	Frank Biela (Audi A4)	289
2	Alain Menu (Renault Laguna)	197
3	Rickard Rydell (Volvo 850)	194
4	David Leslie (Honda Accord)	159
5	Jo Winkelhock (BMW 320i)	158
6	Roberto Ravaglia (BMW 320i)	157

1997

Auto Trader British Touring Car Championship

1	Alain Menu (Renault Laguna)	281
2	Frank Biela (Audi A4)	171
3	Jason Plato (Renault Laguna)	170
4	Rickard Rydell (Volvo S40)	137
5	James Thompson (Honda Accord)	132
6	Gabriele Tarquini (Honda Accord)	130

1998

Auto Trader British Touring Car Championship

1	Rickard Rydell (Volvo S40)	254
2	Anthony Reid (Nissan Primera GT)	239
3	James Thompson (Honda Accord)	203
4	Alan Menu (Renault Laguna)	187
5	Jason Plato (Renault Laguna)	163
6	David Leslie (Nissan Primera GT)	148

1999

Auto Trader British Touring Car Championship

1	Laurent Aiello (Nissan Primera)	244
2	David Leslie (Nissan Primera)	228
3	Rickard Rydell (Volvo S40)	152
4	James Thompson (Honda Accord)	134
5	Jason Plato (Renault Laguna)	122
6	Yvan Muller (Vauxhall Vectra)	119

2000

Auto Trader British Touring Car Championship

1	Alain Menu (Ford Mondeo)	195
2	Anthony Reid (Ford Mondeo)	193
3	Rickard Rydell (Ford Mondeo)	178
4	Yvan Muller (Vauxhall Vectra)	168
5	Jason Plato (Vauxhall Vectra)	160
6	Gabriele Tarquini (Honda Accord)	149

2001

AA/MSA British Touring Car Championship

1	Jason Plato (Vauxhall Astra Coupé)	336
2	Yvan Muller (Vauxhall Astra Coupé)	318
3	James Thompson (Vauxhall Astra Coupé)	276
4	Phil Bennett (Vauxhall Astra Coupé)	173
5	Dan Eaves (Peugeot 406 Coupé)	115
6	Steve Soper (Peugeot 406 Coupé)	93

Production Class:

1	Simon Harrison (Peugeot 306)	227
2	James Kaye (Honda Accord)	220
3	Roger Moen (Peugeot 306)	212

2002

Green Flag/MSA British Touring Car Championship

1	James Thompson (Vauxhall Astra Coupé)	183
2	Yvan Muller (Vauxhall Astra Coupé)	163
3	Matt Neal (Vauxhall Astra Coupé)	145
4	Anthony Reid (MG ZS)	136
5	Andy Priaulx (Honda Civic Type-R)	116
6	Warren Hughes (MG ZS)	110

Production Class:

1	James Kaye (Honda Civic Type-R)	210
2	Norman Simon (BMW 320i)	180
3	Spencer Marsh (Honda Accord)	122

2003

Green Flag/MSA British Touring Car Championship

1	Yvan Muller (Vauxhall Astra Coupé)	233
2	James Thompson (Vauxhall Astra Coupé)	199
3	Matt Neal (Honda Civic Type R)	148
4	Paul O'Neill (Vauxhall Astra Coupé)	138
5	Alan Morrison (Honda Civic Type-R)	125
6	Anthony Reid (MG ZS)	121

Production Class

1	Luke Hines (Honda Civic Type-R)	243
2	Alan Blencowe (Honda Civic Type-R)	193
3	Michael Bentwood (BMW 320i)	186

2004

Green Flag/MSA British Touring Car Championship

1	James Thompson (Vauxhall Astra Coupé)	274
2	Yvan Muller (Vauxhall Astra Coupé)	273
3	Jason Plato (SEAT Toledo Cupra)	224
4	Anthony Reid (MG ZS)	213
5	Matt Neal (Honda Civic Type-R)	181
6	Colin Turkington (MG ZS)	173

2005

Dunlop MSA British Touring Car Championship

1	Matt Neal (Honda Integra Type-R)	316
2	Yvan Muller (Vauxhall Astra Sport Hatch)	273
3	Dan Eaves (Honda Integra Type-R)	269
4	Jason Plato (SEAT Toledo Cupra)	208
5	Tom Chilton (Honda Civic Type-R)	175
6	Colin Turkington (Vauxhall Astra Sport Hatch)	174

2006

Dunlop MSA British Touring Car Championship

1	Matt Neal (Honda Integra Type-R)	289
2	Jason Plato (SEAT Leon)	241
3	Colin Turkington (MG ZS)	240
4	Gordon Shedden (Honda Integra Type-R)	204
5	Fabrizio Giovanardi (Vauxhall Astra Sport Hatch)	163
6	James Thompson (SEAT Leon)	162

2007

Dunlop MSA British Touring Car Championship

1	Fabrizio Giovanardi (Vauxhall Vectra)	300
2	Jason Plato (SEAT Leon)	297
3	Gordon Shedden (Honda Civic)	200
4	Matt Neal (Honda Civic)	195
5	Colin Turkington (BMW 320si)	184
6	Darren Turner (SEAT Leon)	160

AFN 56
Aiello, Laurent 141
Aintree 19, 26
Aitken-Walker, Louise 117, 131
Alan Mann Racing (AMR) 19, 38-39, 44-45, 53-54, 56, 61-62, 73, 75
Alfa Romeo 141, 172, 182
  GTV6 114, 120, 133 147 194 155, 150, 165, 179, 181; Silverstone 140
Allam, Jeff 93, 114, 126, 131
Alvis 8
Appleyard, Ian 8
Arundell, Pete 38, 44, 48
Aston Martin Tickford 115
Audi A4 141, 143, 150, 154, 161, 165, 167, 194
Austin
  A30 8
  A35 9, 18, 25
  A40
  A90 Westminster 9, 14
  A105 Westminster 9, 18, 22
Austin-Rover 114, 123, 126
  Metro 93
  Metro 6R4 114
Autocar magazine 7-9, 77
Autosport magazine 18, 76-77, 141, 195

Baillie, Sir Gawaine 19, 38, 45
Ballisat, Keith 31
Banks, Warwick 37
Bell, Roger 92, 94, 97
Bellm, Ray 171
Bevan, George 76-77, 83
B. F. Goodrich tyres 194
Bianchi, Lucien 56
Biela, Frank 141, 143, 161, 163
Bintcliffe, John 143
Birmingham street circuit 139
Birrell, Gerry 76, 79, 85
Blydenstein, Bill 19
BMC 18-19
  Mini 62, 68; 850 9, 19, 26
  Mini-Cooper 19, 29, 31, 41, 45; S 19, 41, 44-45, 65, 68, 71, 73, 93; 970S 45; 1275GT 92-93, 110; 1275S 19, 37, 45, 47-48, 52, 65, 76
BMC Competition Department 25, 45
BMW 71, 114, 135, 140-141, 143, 161, 163, 171, 176, 182
  CSi 92
  M3 114-115, 135, 140, 182

3.0CSL 77
3 Series 148, 153, 169 318 141; 318i 150, 153; 318is 140, 148 320i 141, 165 530i 93 635CSi 114-115
Borgward Isabella 19, 25
Boss 76, 79
Bradford, Robin 93
Brancatelli, Gianfranco 115
Brands Hatch 18-19, 25, 31, 32, 45, 48, 53, 56, 61, 66, 73, 76-77, 79, 85, 90, 93, 97, 117, 153, 159, 163, 165, 194-195, 212, 220, 224, 227-228
Bristol 8
  401 8
  403 17
Bristow, Laurence 15
Britax 47
British GP 92; 1962 26; 1972 77
British Leyland 47, 68, 109
British Racing & Sports Car Club (BRSCC) 7, 18-19
British Saloon/Touring Car Championship (BTCC) 18; 1958 9, 22; 1959 25; 1962 45; 1964 34; 1965 43; 1966 44; 1967 62; 1968 53; 1970 45, 76, 79, 83; 1971 76-77, 83; 1972 76-77, 83, 88; 1973 77; 1974 76-77, 90, 92, 94; 1975 92, 95, 97, 109, 159; 1976 92; 1977 93; 1978 93, 110; 1979 110, 113; 1980 93, 113; 1981 113; 1983 114, 120, 133, 135, 159; 1984 114, 159; 1985 114-115, 159; 1987 77, 115; 1988 119; 1989 141; 1990 115, 139; 1992 140, 148; 1993 140; 1994 140, 179, 181; 1995 141, 144, 146; 1996 141; 1997 141, 154; 1998 193; 2001 194, 211; 2002 194; 2003 194; 2004 195; 2005 195, 201; 2006 195, 201, 204, 206
BRM 8, 18
Broad, Ralph 50, 92, 94
Broadspeed 37, 44-45, 50, 52-54, 66, 68, 76-77, 85, 87-88, 90, 92-93, 97, 109
Brodie, Dave 77, 114
Brookes, Tony 9
Brooklands 8
Brundle, Martin 93
Buckley, 17
Bueb, Ivor 14, 17-18, 25
Buncombe, Jonathan 76
Burn, Michael 14
Burt, Kelvin 165

Carlisle, Christabel 19, 31, 41
Chambers, Marcus 25
Chevrolet
  Camaro 9, 45, 76-77, 79-80, 85, 88, 92; Z28 92
  Impala 19
Chilton, Tom 204, 231
Chrysler 45, 76, 92-94
  Avenger 93; GT 92-93, 104, 109
Clark, Jim 7, 19, 34, 38-39, 44
Cleland, John 115, 117, 131, 133, 140-141, 143-144, 146, 167, 171, 189
Collard, Rob 206
Colt Starion Turbo 114
Coombs 26
Cooper 19, 41, 68
Cooper, John 47
Crabtree, Mike 45
Craft, Chris 44-45, 52, 76, 87, 102
Crystal Palace 19, 32
Culpan, Norman 8

Daimler Conquest Century 17
Davenport, John 109
Davis, S. C. H. 'Sammy' 8
De Mattos, Basil 17
Derrington, Vic 13
DKW 14
Donington Park 115, 150, 181-182, 189
Dowsett, Phil 133
Dron, Tony 92-93, 104
Dunlop tyres 194

Eaves, Dan 195, 204
Eggenberger 115, 135, 139
Elford, Vic 19, 44, 56, 61
Engines
  BMC A-series 9
  Chevrolet V8 77
  Coventry-Climax 66
  Ford BDA 76-77, 90; V6 184; V8 44-45, 76
  Ford-Cosworth FVA 44-45, 53, 56, 59, 66
  Mountune 115
  Riley 8
  Sodemo 194
  Triumph 92
England, 'Lofty' 9, 18
Equipe Arden 45
Equipe Endeavour 18
ERA 8
European Touring Car Championship 1988 115
Fabris, 'Edgy' 18
Fearnall, Robert 77
FIA 9, 92, 140, 195
Fiat 500 8

Fittipaldi, Emerson 77
Fitzpatrick, John 44-45, 50, 52, 54, 76-77, 85, 87, 117
Ford 8-9, 13, 18, 41, 50, 56, 68, 85, 87, 93, 101, 114, 140-141
  Anglia 8, 44, 50, 62, 66; 100E 14; 105E 18, 44, 50, 65; 1-litre 45; 1200 19; 1.3 45, 50, 68; Super 50, 65
  Capri 77, 88, 92, 101-102, 114, 120; RS2600 76-77, 79, 83; 3000GT 7, 9, 93, 104, 113; II 92-93, 99, 102; III 92-93, 101-102, 104
  Consul 13, 17
  Cortina GT 9, 19, 32
  Escort 45, 54, 56, 59, 62, 73, 92, 123; RS 87; RS Turbo 114-115, 123, 126; RS1600 76-77, 85, 87-88, 90, 114, 123; Twin-Cam 45, 48, 53-54, 56, 61, 66, 73, 76, 87; 1300GT 45, 52-54, 73, 76-77, 85, 88
  Falcon 9, 19, 39, 43-45, 47-48, 54, 61-62, 66, 68, 71, 75
  Galaxie 9-10, 19, 32, 34, 41, 44-45, 68, 71
  Merkur Sierra XR4Ti 114-115, 117, 120
  Mondeo 140-141, 150, 153-154, 159, 169, 182, 184, 194
  Mustang 19, 38-39, 43, 45, 47, 54, 68, 76, 79
  Sierra 114; RS500 Cosworth 7, 9, 45, 77, 114-115, 117, 119, 135, 139-140, 159, 195
  Zephyr 8-9, 13-14, 18, 22; Mk II 9, 25
  Zodiac Mk III 31
Ford-Germany 43
Ford Mexico Series 77
Ford Motorsport 77, 92
Fortescue-Thomas, Gillian 77, 90
Foster, 31
Fraser, Alan 44-45, 66
Fraser Nash 8

Gardner, Frank 44-45, 48, 53, 56, 59, 61-62, 66, 73, 75-77, 80, 83, 88
Gartlan, Malcolm 77, 80
Giovanardi, Fabrizio 195, 231
GM 140
Goode, Graham 114-115
Goodwood 19, 25, 41, 47

Goodwood Revival Meeting 68, 71
Gow, Alan 194-195
Grace, 'Gib' 9
Grahame, Stuart 92
Grant, Gregor 18
Gravette, Rob 114-115, 119, 139
Group A 7, 93, 114-115, 123, 125, 133
Group 1 76-77, 92, 94, 114
Group 11/2 7, 92-93, 101, 104, 110
Group 2 18-19, 39, 41, 44-45, 76-77, 79, 114
Group 5 7, 9, 19, 39, 43-45, 47-48, 53-54, 56, 62, 65-66, 68, 71, 73, 76, 140
Gurney, Dan 19

Hahne, Hubert 73
Hall, Pete 114
Handley, John 37, 68
Hansgen, Walt 22
Hanson, Peter 77, 90
Harper, Peter 19, 29, 31
Harrison, Ian 195
Harvey, Tim 115, 140, 148
Hawkins, Paul 61
Hawthorn, Mike 9, 17, 21
Haynes, David 25, 31
Healey 8
  Elliot 8
  Tickford 8
Hedges, 31
Hill, Graham 19
Hillman 76
  Avenger GT 92
  Imp 44, 66
  Rallye Imp 44-45
Hine, John 45
Hobbs, David 45
Hodgetts, Chris 115
Holden Commodore 115
Holman & Moody 19
Honda 141, 182, 215, 223, 227
  Accord 141, 143, 154, 171-172, 174, 182, 194
  Civic Type-R 194-195, 201, 204, 220
  Integra Type-R 195, 199, 201, 204, 206
Hopkirk, Paddy 29
Hoy, Will 140, 148, 159, 169
Hughes, Warren 194, 197, 208
Hutcheson, Alan 32
Hutton, Ray 77

Ickx, Jacky 44

Jacobs, Dick 9
Jaguar 7-11, 14, 22, 25, 32, 68, 71, 109
  D-type 9
  Mk II 9, 18-19, 68;

3.8 32, 34
    Mk VII 8-10, 17; Mk VIIM
        9, 13, 17-18
    XJS 114
    XK120
    3.4-litre 17-18, 21-22, 25
Janes, Bob 26
Janspeed 140
Johnson, Leslie 8
Jowett
    Javelin 8
    Jupiter 8

Knockhill 203, 231
Kox, Peter 172

Lammers, Jan 190
Lee, Vic 140
Leslie, David 141
Lexus IS200 194
Lincoln Cars 18
Lloyd, Richard 93, 110
Longman, Richard 76,
    92, 110, 114-115, 123,
    125-126
Lotus-Cortina 7, 9, 19, 32,
    34, 38-39, 44-45, 48, 54,
    56, 68, 71, 73; Mk II 44,
    61, 66
Love, John 19, 29
Lovett, Peter 93, 114

Mallory Park 59, 97
Mann, Alan 54
Mansfield, Rod 45, 87
Markey, John 92
Marshall, Gerry 92-93, 99
Matthews, Dave 76-77, 88
Mays, Raymond 8, 18
Mazda
    Xedos 6 140, 153
    RX3 92, 97
    RX7 92-93, 113
    323 140
McGovern, Bill 76-77,
    83, 88
McLaren, Bruce 19
McLaren, Chris 19
Menu, Alain 141, 159, 163,
    176, 182, 184
Mercedes-Benz 114
MG 8
    Metro 114; Turbo 123
    ZA Magnette 9, 25
    100 31
MG-Rover 194, 197, 227
    ZS 194-195, 197, 203,
    206, 208, 216, 220, 223,
    228
Michelin tyres 9, 18, 184
Miller, Sydney 92
Mini-Cooper 9
Mond, S. 8
Monte Carlo Rally 45, 47-
    48, 54; 1956 14; 1964 44

Moore, Don 18
Morbidelli, Gianni 193
Morris Minor 8
Moss, Stirling 8-11
Motor magazine 94
Muir, Brian 45, 76-77,
    79-80
Muller, Yvan 171, 189,
    194-195, 204, 211-212,
    215, 219-220, 227-228
Mylchreest, B. 8

NASCAR 19, 195
Neal, Matt 169, 194-195,
    199, 201, 204, 219,
    220
Neerpasch, Jochen 43
Nicholson, Mike 194
Nissan 140
    Bluebird Turbo 114
    Primera 154, 161, 194;
        GT 140
    Skyline 115

O'Brian, Mike 115
O'Dell, Des 76, 92
Oliver, Jackie 45
O'Neill, Paul 215
Oulton Park 19, 29, 32,
    52, 101, 120, 212, 215
    Gold Cup race 19, 29

Parkes, Mike 19
Parnell, Reg 17
Paul Ricard 6-hour race
    1972 83
Pearson, Barry 45
Pembrey 153
Pepper, Brian 93
Percy, Win 92-93, 113, 123
Peugeot 141, 181-182
    203 13
    405 146, 153;
    406 141, 154, 169;
        Coupé 194
Phillips, C. B. 8
Pierpoint, Roy 19, 38, 43,
    45, 66
Piper 76
Pirelli tyres 115
Plato, Jason 194-195, 201,
    204, 208, 211-212, 227
Poole, Alec 45
Pond, Tony 114, 123
Porsche 44, 56
    911 44-45, 61
Potter, Len 13
Priaulx, Andy 220
Prodrive 141, 154, 159,
    172, 184
Proton 194, 223

RAC 18, 45, 76, 92, 94,
    125, 135
RAC MSA 7, 44-45, 76-77,
    92-93, 104, 114, 140

Radisich, Paul 140-141,
    150, 154
Reid, Anthony 141, 184,
    194-195, 197, 216
Renault 140-141, 153, 182
    Laguna 140-141, 143,
    146, 150, 154, 163, 182,
    194
Rhodes, John 44-45, 62
Riley 9, 18
    Pathfinder 8-9
    RM 8
    RMC 8, 17
    1.5 19, 32
Rockingham 232
Rolt, Tony 8, 14
Rootes Group 44-45, 66
Rouse, Andy 77, 92-94, 97,
    109, 114-115, 117, 119-
    120, 133, 135, 139-141,
    146, 148, 153, 159, 161
Rover
    Vitesse 114-115, 120,
    126, 129, 131, 133, 135
    SD1 7, 93, 113
    3500 93
Rydell, Rickard 141, 148,
    165, 190, 193

Salvadori, Roy 25
Savory, Ted 41
Saward, Joe 114
Schnitzer 141
Scott-Brown, Archie 17
Sears, Jack 9-10, 18-19,
    22, 26, 32, 43, 117
SEAT 195, 201, 227
    Leon 195, 201, 204, 231
    Toledo Cupra 204, 227
Shawcross, Lord 114
Shedden, Gordon 199, 204
Shepherd, G. C. 'Doc' 18
Silverstone 7-11, 13-14,
    17-19, 21-22, 38, 41, 54,
    56, 61, 68, 73, 88, 99,
    102, 109, 119, 131, 154,
    165, 187
    National Circuit 143
Simoni, Giampiero 117
Smith, Mike 115
Snetterton 19, 34, 76, 117,
    176, 219
Soper, Steve 114-115, 126,
    129, 131, 135, 139-140,
    148, 171, 182
Sopwith, Tommy 18,
    21-22, 43
Special Touring Cars 135
Spice, Gordon 92-93, 99,
    101-102, 104
Sponsors
    AA 194
    Auto Trader 148
    Castrol 94, 99
    Daily Express 8-9
    Datapost 114, 123, 125

Esso 90, 115
    Green Flag 194
    Halfords 195, 199, 201,
    204
    Hammons Chop Sauce
    102
    Hermetite 99
    ICS 114
    Kaliber 135, 139
    Keith Prowse 92
    Labatt's 163
    Laystall 17
    Listerine 140, 169
    SCA Freight 76-77,
    79-80, 88
    Southern Organs 92
    Wiggins Teape 76
Sprinzel, John 9
Spurring, Quentin 76
Stewart, Jackie 87, 126
Stock, Tim 92
Sunbeam 29
    Imp 76-77
    Rallye Imp 76, 83, 88,
    93
    Rapier 9, 18-19, 29, 31
    Texaco 135
    Tiger 93
Sunbeam-Talbot 8
Super 2000 cars 195
SuperTura Championship
    18
Superspeed 44, 50, 52,
    65, 68
Super Touring Cars 7, 9,
    115 140-141, 143, 153,
    159, 167, 174, 189, 194
Sytner, Frank 114-115, 117,
    135

Tarquini, Gabriele 140-141,
    172, 179, 181-182
Taylor, Anita 50
Taylor, Dennis 19
Team Lotus 19, 39, 44, 61
Thompson, James 146,
    171-172, 174, 194-195,
    211-212, 219-220, 227
Thruxton 76, 133, 135, 139
Titterington, Desmond 14
TOCA (Touring Car
    Association) 140-141,
    146, 154
Tom Walkinshaw Racing
    (TWR) 92, 113-114, 120,
    126, 129, 131, 133, 135,
    140-141, 190
Tour de France 38, 54
Tourist Trophy 125; 1970
    80, 87; 1987 119
Toyota 140-141
    Carina 140, 146, 148, 159
    Celica 110; GT 92-93,
    115, 133; Supra 123
    Corolla 115, 133
Trakstar 115, 119, 139

Triple Eight 141, 194
Triumph 93
    Dolomite Sprint 92-94,
    97, 104, 109
Turkington, Colin 194-195,
    203, 206, 228
Tyrrell, Ken 29

Unett, Bernard 66, 92-94,
    104, 109
Uren, Jeff 18, 22, 25, 31

Vandervell, Colin 92
Vauxhall 8, 99, 117,
    135, 140-141, 181-182,
    189, 197, 215-216, 220,
    223, 227, 231
    Astra 115, 141, 206, 208,
    232; Coupé 194-195,
    208, 211-212, 215,
    223; GT/E 117, 131,
    133; Sport Hatch 195,
    204, 228, 231
    Cavalier 140-141, 144,
    146, 150, 153, 163, 169
    Magnum 93; Coupé 92,
    99, 104
    Vectra 141, 143-144,
    154, 167, 169, 171,
    189, 194, 195
Volvo 125, 140-141, 167
    S40 141, 193-194
    850 141, 146, 148, 165;
    850SE estate 140, 190,
    193
VW
    Golf GTI 93, 109, 131
    Scirocco 110

Walker, Peter 8
Walkinshaw, Tom 93, 99,
    104, 113-114, 140
Warwick, Derek 17
Watts, Patrick 140
Weaver, James 115
Webb, John 195
Weslake, Harry 18
West, Richard 194
West Surrey Racing (WSR)
    194, 197
Wharton, Ken 8-9, 13-14
Whitmore, Sir John 19, 29,
    34, 43
Williams F1 141
Williams, Barrie 92
Willment 32
Winkelhock, Jo 140-141,
    161, 165
Woodman, Vince 76-77, 88,
    90, 92
World Touring Car
    Championship 1987 115;
    Challenge 1993 140

Yokohama tyres 115
Young, John 18
Young, Mike 44, 65